STARTING A SMALL
RESTAURANT

A Guide to Excellence
in the Purveying
of Public Victuals

Revised Edition

DANIEL MILLER

The Harvard Common Press
HARVARD AND BOSTON, MASSACHUSETTS

The Harvard Common Press
535 Albany Street
Boston, Massachusetts 02118

Printed in the United States of America.

Library of Congress Cataloging in Publication Data

Miller, Daniel, 1932–
    Starting a small restaurant.

    Includes index.
    1. Restaurant management.   I. Title.
TX911.3.M27M54   1983   647'.95'068   83-6188
ISBN 0-916782-38-7
ISBN 0-916782-37-9 (pbk.)

Cover design by Peter Good

10

To Shirley,
who has something special
from start to finish.

Acknowledgments

This book could never have been if not for Shirley; Hilda Steele; Sheree; Abe and Ruth; Becky, Scott, and Mike; Andy and Jack Herrington; Jim Harris; Ken Kelly; Del Stanton; David Megibow; Brian and Sylvia Hume; Mabel Souza; Warren Leopold; Karen Gunther Theisz; Wilfred Lyons; Paul and Louise Squibb; Bob Doerr; Warren Talcott; Robert May, R.N.; Leslie; Ed and Kathleen; the 1971 San Fernando earthquake; Cambria, California, and a cast of thousands. But they didn't write it.

Contents

Introduction

HAVE you tried a local, family-run restaurant recently? If you enjoyed it, compare it with what is described in this book. But if you found the place unsatisfactory, perhaps you can discover in these pages examples of what should have been done. If so, I urge you to strike a blow for restaurant customers everywhere by returning to the place to give it another chance. Take this book with you. If the restaurant has not improved, leave the book with the owner when you send back your uneaten meal. Then go home, instead of to another restaurant. Have a glass of wine, relax, and you'll feel better about the experience. (Doing without the meal is good for you. Besides, you will probably already have eaten an appetizer or a salad or soup, so you won't starve.) Then resolve to open your own restaurant—or to buy the place you just visited and improve it.

I have a theory about small restaurants and their unique role in today's stressful American society. They provide the public with one of the last vestiges of true enterprise and inventiveness left in our corporate concentration camp. A small restaurant is one of the few places where the distraught parents of small children can regain their sanity and feelings of romance, where the weary traveler can feel truly at home, where a family can enjoy each other's company but not have to do the dishes, and where the owner's hard work and love of excellence shows. Once it discovers one of these good small restaurants, the public really is appreciative and supportive. The place may eventually change, expand beyond control, go out of business, or fail to maintain quality—but the customer always retains the choice whether to patronize it. What matters in the long run is that such places can continue to spring up, like good mushrooms.

This book is for anyone who has thought about opening a small restaurant, or who has a friend who wants to do so. It is my purpose here to try to make it a little less scary for people without professional restaurant experience to be good mushrooms. Like the lowly mushroom, the small restaurant, if prepared properly, can overcome even an inauspicious beginning and add a unique and distinctive flavor to life.

Starting a Small Restaurant

1. So You Think You Should Open a Restaurant?

YOU have always wanted to open a little restaurant. And good ones are in demand almost everywhere. But those who aspire to cook for and serve the discerning restaurant patron must survive pitfalls as many and varied as the people who open restaurants, and the places that need them. The purpose of this opening chapter is, frankly, to discourage you from acting out your fantasy—or someone else's. All your friends, who have just been treated to another of your wonderfully warm parties with delicious food and drinks, are urging you to open your own little place. Do not listen to them. Not unless you realize many years will pass before you will spend another full evening with them, either as host or guest.

Are you the sort of person who looks forward to a two- or three-day weekend when you can forget your workday chores and do something different, exciting, out-of-town? Forget that. When you run a restaurant, even if you serve an industrial park clientele weekday breakfast and lunch, either you will be too tired to enjoy an active weekend, or you will find unfinished work that takes up much weekend time. And beware: when the government contracts that enable your industrial clientele to eat out begin to get shaky, your loyal customers will "brown bag" you to oblivion.

Perhaps you have been thinking for several years about how it will be when you get your own place and "run it right." Well, you have persistence, and that is a good sign. You will need more than you imagined. Let's review some of the more discouraging aspects of the restaurant business first. Hold on tight.

THE IMPORTANCE OF LOCATION

Where will you open your restaurant? If you live in a city, one place is as bad as another, or as good. A surprising number of factors are relevant—neighborhood, proximity of other attractions, transportation, parking, zoning, previous occupancy, and ownership or lease-hold, to name a few. Once you decide what location you would prefer, be prepared to go through the selection process again because some silly landlord has an inflated view of the value of his property. Invariably, the landlord believes he is doing *you* a favor by letting you open a wonderful restaurant in his shopping center, or by letting you remodel his fifty-year-old building on Decrepit Street. Rest assured—he will ask, nay, demand, an unrealistic rental. Should he happen to own a building of previous restaurant occupancy and some of the equipment is still in it, he will offer to let you rent the whole package for a mere pittance—12 percent of your gross monthly sales or $2,500, whichever is greater. Don't let the garlic get in your eyes, as they say in Palermo. If the equipment is as old as it looks (and he has already depreciated it to zero) maybe you can make a better deal by purchasing the workable stuff. But more on that later.

> *Having a good sense of humor will not guarantee your success in this business, but it doesn't hurt. A prominent restaurateur once told me, "My people are always having either a 'day off' or an 'off day.'" A few years earlier, one of his employees who was having an "off day" shot him. With luck this won't happen to you. If it does, try to keep your sense of humor.*

Location isn't everything, you say. Yes, but it is a lot—preferably with a nice building. If you cannot rely on walk-in trade, because no one ever walks past your restaurant, you will partly lose the opportunity to show how good you are while you are still young. You cannot rely on a sign where people are driving by; nobody will notice it unless it is ugly, and if it is, do you want it? If you will rely on word-of-mouth recommendations, your location must not be impossible to explain to an exhausted traveler on the telephone, an octogenarian from the Midwest, or the lady to whom all gas stations look alike. In short, location is so important that part of the next chapter is devoted to the subject in detail.

Unless you are very rich, you cannot simply open your pride and joy just anywhere. Selecting the place to change your life is a matter for serious consideration in advance. Your final decision on undertaking the whole crazy idea must hinge on whether you can get the location and type of building you want.

CHANGING YOUR LIFE STYLE

Your decision to go ahead with this restaurant project augurs a change in your way of life that you may actually anticipate with pleasure. Perhaps you will move out of the city to your old home town where the schools are less crowded, or to a resort community in a lovely spot. But are you ready to make the change from a steady, familiar job with biweekly paychecks, a credit union, and group health and life insurance, to becoming a small business operator who cannot have even workers' compensation in case you accidentally serve your fingertip in a Caesar salad? Are you ready to switch from eating your own or your spouse's cooking, with its nice variety of dishes to suit your respective moods, to a choice of leftovers from tonight's efforts? There are advantages to being the only good restaurant in the small town in which you have chosen to make your culinary mark. But if yours is the only good eating place in town, you are one of the losers when you want to eat out on your night off. And, believe me, you must have a night off. You will want to eat someone else's cooking on that night whether or not you are the chef at your place. Possibly you will be rescued by a reasonably good place in an adjacent town, but don't count on it.

Do you have school-age children? Unless you serve breakfast and lunch only, you will not see the children much after school; in the evenings when you serve dinner you will be too busy. You may think you can compensate for the loss of time with your child as other working parents do; but the restaurant business is too all-consuming to allow that dream to become a reality, if both parents are actively engaged in the business. Ponder this: without exception, every grown-up I asked whose parents had a restaurant when they were children said they would never run one themselves! Does that tell you something? Of course, you may be the rare parent who does not expect more from his children than they are willing to give. Or your children may be the kind who are so sensitive to your needs as overworked owners of a restaurant that they lighten your burden without really being asked. But it doesn't make it any easier for you to see your sweet child forego the pleasure of a Saturday night dance or a ski trip because it is a busy weekend at the family restaurant and one of your best waitresses is visiting a sick grandmother in Utah.

You will not know the true meaning of the word "exhaustion" until you have opened your own restaurant.

Let it be understood at the outset: Your life style will alter in such basic and drastic ways that you may not recognize that you have a life at all. Just a restaurant. Some people solve that problem, to an extent, by remaining open only Thursday through Sunday. Such hours allow two or three days for a little life of sorts. Others solve it by closing or selling out after a couple of years. Some just get sick and die. Some even burn the place down and collect the insurance, if any, or go to jail. (There's a life style change!) I suppose there are other solutions. You may come up with a good one.

I leave this topic with one thought more. No one but another restaurant person will ever understand why you refuse to remain open seven days per week, serving three meals per day. And when you are asked by an overwrought motel manager why you close Mondays *and* Tuesdays, you will learn to answer in a steady voice and to keep your hands in your pockets where the questioner cannot see your clenched fists. Luckily for both of you, it is hard to whip your fists out of most pockets.

There is something about the pleasure of eating a home-cooked meal served in a friendly manner by a happy person that evokes memories of childhood. The best part is that it is a happy experience, even if your childhood wasn't.

YOUR PERSONALITY

Wanting to open a restaurant says something about you right off the bat. You have a strong character; you are creative; and you seek independence. Your own restaurant will offer you a number of opportunities to express your unique talents. The decor and ambience of your place, the wines, the style of service, and, of course, the menu and taste of the food will all reflect you as a person, your heritage, and your own likes and dislikes. Having recognized all the foregoing when you decided to proceed, you need now only reflect on a few other aspects of restaurant life.

Have you ever had to put up with your partner for so many hours per day? Can you stand to listen to each other discuss the business during much of your other time together, at least at first? Probably most restaurant owners (or any business partners), especially those who live together, learn to avoid constant discussion of problems and unfinished business during off hours. But in the beginning, when there is so little free time, it is unavoidable. Are you wise enough to escape the disastrous consequences?

The women's movement has spawned a number of successful restaurants. This is not surprising, because independent, strong-willed people have been opening restaurants for years. And women have been drawn to the challenge of expanding their cooking experience into a money-earning profession as a way toward independence or self-support. What is new is the extent of cooperation among women owners of restaurants and their female employees, whereby aspects of exploitation are eliminated and somewhat more profit sharing occurs. It will be interesting to see if such ventures have a longer life than most small restaurants. One restaurant catering to women in the Boston area eliminated the traditional server role and the need for tipping, which reduced the cost of the meal for the clientele. The patron was served water, a menu, and an order pad by a kitchen employee. When decided, the customer took the order to the counter, and was later notified when the meal was ready for pickup. It may not qualify as elegance, but it worked—until recently, anyway, when the place closed.

Being a restaurateur doesn't exempt you from ordinary people's family life problems; in many respects, it will exacerbate those that already exist. If you have a good communication of feelings in your relationship, it will be a little easier to cope. If you don't, but think you do, try talking about all the reasons why you want to make the drastic changes you are contemplating. Is it to express your creativity and realize greater independence, or are you just tired of each other?

Let's suppose you have and can keep a strong, loving relationship that will weather the coming storms. How do you get along with the public? Have you ever had to, in your previous business or occupation? You will have little choice about it in your new profession. Either you must run so excellent a restaurant that you can afford to be eccentric and reject all those customers whose behavior you will not tolerate, or you will have to tolerate. And tolerate all kinds. Drunks who appear sober as they enter and are seated will then begin to abuse the server or the nice people at the next table. Militant anti-smokers can get into a vitriolic spat with militant smokers. Middle-Eastern connoisseurs of lamb who hate your loin lamb chops will say so in a very loud voice some frantic Saturday night. There are innumerable wise guys who complain vociferously about a tough steak *after* they have eaten all of it. There are madmen who call you in the midst of a madhouse evening to ask you what your hours are for Sunday brunch and what sort of food you specialize in. There is an entire tribe who travel around and always come in at 11:15 a.m.—fifteen minutes after you've stopped serving the breakfast menu. They insist on having poached eggs rather than any of the delicious items on your luncheon menu.

Employee relations also require consummate skill. Picture your quiet, perhaps elegant dining room and your demure new waitress who started work yesterday and is still scared to death. A former waitress—a regular Valkyrie—who expected to be rehired when business picked up for the summer, declaims loudly in a fit of pique when Fraidy Cat approaches her table, *"This place stinks! They were supposed to hire me back!"* A few minutes later, still shaken, you discover that the long-haired, pimply-faced dishwasher, whom you have repeatedly warned to keep his hands out of the food, is still sneaking handfuls of grated cheese.

In other words, are you ready for public and employee relations at their most nitty gritty? Think about it. A long time.

MANAGING THE MONEY

How are you at handling money? The cash flow of a restaurant can be very deceiving to the new businessperson. By simply looking at large receipts from a busy day's effort you may conclude that you have made a good profit, when in fact you barely broke even. In seasonal locations it is very easy for you to forget, in the middle of booming business, that right after Labor Day everything comes to a screeching halt. It is terribly easy to become overextended.

For every dollar of employee wages paid you must set aside at least another ten cents to cover the employer's portion of Social Security, unemployment, and disability insurance, not to mention workers' compensation, withholding taxes, and other hidden overhead costs. Will you be collecting state sales tax in your state? The quarterly and yearly forms on which you must report all of the above seem endless and often incomprehensible, especially when you start trying to decide from a government publication whether or not to include tips and employee meals when computing the figure called for by some particular form. And the form requires you to differentiate between your regular employees and your own minor children, who are exempt from certain taxes. The bookkeeper will do it, you say? Yes, but who will check on the bookkeeper? And can you afford a certified public accountant when you are first getting started? (Can you afford *not* to have a C.P.A. is a much better question.)

If there are to be two managers for your restaurant, whether spouses or partners, how well do you two agree on money matters? Do you have the same goals for using your money if you make a profit? For example, will one of you wisely intend to reinvest some of your profits to make needed improvements in the place, only to discover after a year of hard work that the other one wants to take a much-needed cruise to the Caribbean? Are you ready for the old ice machine to break down again, or can you spend the twelve hundred dollars necessary for a new one, which will take a little bit longer to break down? Money differences are probably the easiest problems to solve when everything else is going well, but they are also the root of many evils in a restaurant. After all, you are trying to make a lot of money with all that creativity; and you really don't want to share it with anyone who doesn't deserve it, right? Maybe you feel that you work a lot harder than your partner. That sentiment alone is enough to break up a good partnership. Don't start thinking that it is your partner's fault that you didn't get what you expected or that you did what you never intended to do.

If you must borrow money to start your restaurant, pay it back on schedule, without fail. If you are not certain of your own ability to repay the loan, try to do without it. And be wary of whom you approach to finance your plans. Invariably, the wealthy person who is ready to lend money or invest in a good enterprise will end up trying to tell you just how to run it.

You have plenty of hard thinking to do before you take the plunge. But if you can answer "yes" to all of the following questions, it is probably safe to go ahead with your plans to open a small restaurant.

- Are there important goals for which you are willing to work extremely hard—in addition to the desire for money—that you will fulfill by opening your own restaurant?
- Are you and your family ready for drastic but potentially exciting changes in your life style?
- Are you (and your partner) willing to take a major personal risk while you determine whether or not you have what it takes to make your new career work?
- Do you have any related experience, or a trusted adviser who has it?
- Do you have a good idea of the type of food you will be best at serving, and does the public in the area where you wish to locate need a restaurant serving that food?
- Do you have enough capital to start a high-risk business and survive the first difficult years?

2. Getting Ready To Do It

S O WHERE do you start, once you have made the decision to change your life? Do not start by buying restaurant equipment. There are a few important steps you should take before you commit yourself to any specific location. The only investment these steps require is your own time and effort.

- Get restaurant experience, if you and your partner have never previously worked in commercial food service jobs.
- Prepare your tentative meal plans and menus. This is a prerequisite for site selection, determining your equipment needs, and discussions with advisers.
- Visit equipment dealers and auctions to learn about all the types of equipment available and the likely capital outlay.

GET RESTAURANT EXPERIENCE

Are you really qualified to operate your own restaurant? Have you or has anyone in your family ever worked at any aspect of food service? Cafeteria work in college is not good enough. It is a rare school cafeteria where anyone actually cares whether the customer got his money's worth. Be realistic. If you have never cooked, or been a server, or worked in the kitchen or dining room of a commercial eating place, you had better get a job doing just that before you proceed any further. There is no substitute for direct experience.

Even in a bad restaurant, you will learn a great deal of value to you. If you use your eyes and nose, you might learn what it means not to keep a clean kitchen. You can learn to appreciate a refrigerator that smells good, and to understand the need for vermin control. But the most important lesson is the value of teamwork in all aspects of restaurant operation, and the necessity for developing step-saving habits. Restaurant people are vulnerable to the effects of long hours and hard work on their legs, feet, and backs. The properly planned kitchen and dining room are really designed to minimize the incidence of varicose veins, midnight leg cramps, and chronic lower back pain.

If possible, once you have your job, spend time doing many different tasks in the place, even if you have to volunteer. Work as a busperson or dishwasher to start with. Move into serving or assisting in the kitchen, if you can. In each job, no matter how physically demanding, you will learn the effects of good or poor teamwork. If possible, work for at least a week at each position, and preferably for several weeks. Never hesitate to help the dishwasher if you are a busperson or server. Stay an extra half hour after your shift (or arrive half an hour early) to help in the kitchen, just to pick up the feel of working there. You will undoubtedly reap a double benefit. Your coworkers and employer will appreciate your helpfulness and concern.

> *Panic among kitchen personnel is best avoided by team-work, encouragement, humor, and leadership from the seasoned veterans of past panics. The chef is the key to this process.*

How long should you work in someone else's restaurant? That depends on your own family circumstances and your success in finding a good location for your own place. But, in fairness to your employer (if you are working for pay rather than volunteering at a friend's place), you should plan on being there for at least four months. It takes three to six months for an inexperienced employee to be fully broken in at any restaurant.

YOUR MENU DETERMINES YOUR INCOME

It may seem premature to try to set your menu and operating hours at this early stage, but there are good reasons for doing so. What you serve at your restaurant will determine what you can earn and spend; you should make up a tentative menu to establish in your mind how extensive the operation will be. This exercise will assist you in answering questions from equipment people, from owners of possible restaurant sites, and from small business advisers. It will also form the basis for your initial discussions with local food suppliers.

Once you have decided on the kinds of meals you will serve, and whether or not you will serve beer and wine or liquor, you must set an approximate price range for your meals. Then you can make an estimate of the expected gross income, which in turn will determine your building rental or purchase budget.

Your prices should be competitive with those of other restaurants in the general area, even if you plan to serve a different kind of food. Obviously, at this early stage you will have to use rough figures for factors like the number of tables you will have and the number of meals per day you will serve. Estimate these numbers conservatively, and then project your weekly gross intake and your monthly and yearly gross, based on how many weeks per year you plan to operate.

For example, let us assume that you will have between fifteen and twenty-five tables, and that the typical day will result in five meals per table. If the average price of a meal with beverage is $9, and you operate six days per week for eleven months of the year, then:

20 tables x 5 meals x $9 = $900 daily gross income
$900 x 6 days x 48 weeks = $259,200 yearly gross income

If you use the standard rule of thumb that up to 7 percent of your gross income can be spent for rent, or for loan retirement and property taxes, then you should budget about $18,000 per year for that purpose. This subject is treated more extensively in Chapter 11.

If you find an especially good location that might increase your chances of serving more meals per table per day, a higher rent budget may be justified. You might assume that a larger amount of usable dining room space would also justify higher rent. But this is not always the case. Remember, you want to open a small restaurant so you can keep tight control. You might decide to make part of the space into a private dining room or banquet facility, and then attract business for it. Catering to banquets, however, is not always worth the added headaches; it will not be lucrative unless there is a great demand for such facilities in the area. And when the separate room is not needed for a group, it may be difficult to use it for regular dining.

If you happen to find a particularly good building with more space than you need for your dining room, you can consider creating a related business enterprise in the extra space. A small jewelry or gift shop, an art gallery, or a boutique might do well, for example. A retail outlet for special food items such as baked goods could be established. Or you might set up a separate dessert and ice cream shop to serve those who eat dinner at home but like to go out for dessert. Maybe you could open a wine and cheese or coffee bar. Use your imagination. But remember that most such enterprises will contribute little toward paying the rent. The cost of labor to cover the operation will swallow up most of the income, at least at the beginning.

LEARN ABOUT RESTAURANT EQUIPMENT

Eventually you will not be able to put off any longer becoming familiar with the equipment you will need to operate your place. Your menu plans will determine your equipment requirements.

Of these, the most critical items are refrigeration and cooking/baking units; dishwashing, work space, and storage run close behind. And overshadowing all is the proper layout of the equipment to allow the food to be placed handily on serving dishes, picked up by the server, and delivered to the hungry customer as efficiently as possible.

Other restaurants' kitchens. With this in mind, you can learn a lot by viewing kitchens in other restaurants. If you take the time to make prior arrangements, you will be allowed to see the kitchen in a good restaurant at a time convenient for the staff. Do not ask to see it while it is in actual operation; and do not ask for "a peek at the kitchen" right after your meal. You want a short but hard look; but be sure to mention that your concern is to see the particular layout, rather than to inspect for cleanliness. The manager of the restaurant will be more disposed to honor your request if you ask after making a reservation for dinner or lunch. And you had better reassure him that the restaurant you are thinking of opening will be in some distant city.

When you get into the kitchen, avoid asking questions to which the answers are obvious from careful observation. Do not hesitate, though, to ask the manager, chef, or server what are the special disadvantages of that layout and what improvements they would make if they could. It is wise to draw a quick sketch from memory after you leave, or perhaps a companion could do it while you are in the kitchen.

Equipment auctions and dealers. By first visiting restaurant equipment dealers and auctions, you can become familiar with all kinds of equipment while having a lot of fun with your fantasies. Restaurant equipment auctions take place periodically in most large cities; check the classified section of your newspaper. Before the day of the auction, visit the people who run the show for an inspection of the wares. Unless he is selling off the equipment right from the premises of a closed place, the auctioneer usually operates by maintaining a warehouse where he refurbishes the equipment between auctions. If you get to know him a little, he may show you the goods in the condition they arrive in. You will learn something from that—mostly how hard it is to find a good cleanup and maintenance person for your restaurant. If the auctioneer is a competent and honest businessman, he takes pains to discover the obvious faults or missing parts of the equipment, and although you will bid on it "as is, where is," he should acknowledge shortcomings at the time it goes on the block. A refrigerator should become demonstrably cold if you ask to see it plugged in during the pre-auction inspection period. An ice-maker should make ice. And so on.

Unscrupulous dealers. At any reliable auction, you will be bidding against local dealers in used equipment. If you frequent the auctions or the dealers' own places, you will learn to recognize them. Sometimes they will identify themselves to you in an insidious way.

Suppose you are the unsuccessful bidder on a nice stainless-steel double sink with left and right drainboards, an eighteen-inch backsplash, and a built-in disposer/grinder. You bid $550 and it was sold to the highest bidder at $625. Shortly thereafter a man appears at your elbow telling you quietly that he has an even better sink at his store, which he will be happy to let you have for the price you bid. Invariably his interruption causes you to lose track of the bidding on the next item, which you really needed because it was just the right size for your place and in excellent condition. It is best to learn to ignore such people. It is unlikely that he will sell you an equivalent item at close to the auction selling price. Worse yet, he will almost always overstate the condition of his goods; if you take the time to go look at them, you will probably be disappointed.

A soup pot burner looks small and practical when you first see one. But unless you are planning to serve mostly soup and must make it in fifty-gallon batches, don't buy one. The burner sits low where it can easily torch an apron, and it takes up valuable space under the hood that is not really usable for anything but a very large pot.

If your friend the unscrupulous dealer is a first-class creep, he will approach you casually when you are the successful bidder on a big item and snidely mention that he has an even better one you could have bought from him for $100 less. The kindest thing you can do is to ignore such dealing. It is unethical for a dealer to take advantage of the auctioneer's advertising and effort as a means of garnering customers right on the auction premises. If you feel annoyed enough, you can ask the auctioneer to throw the bum out.

It is always possible that a dealer or another buyer at the auction really does have an item that you need and that escaped you in the bidding. He will seek you out toward the end of the auction or at a moment when it will not disturb you, and will discreetly arrange for you to see what he has. You will be able to discern from his manner and approach whether it might be worthwhile to pursue the offer.

EVALUATE POSSIBLE SITES

Now you are ready to do the work necessary to find a location for your own restaurant. Of all you will do to ensure success, this groundwork means the most. It may spell the difference between great satisfaction and just a lot of hard work for not much reward.

- Choose the area in which you believe your type of restaurant will do well.
- Investigate all business-related plans for the area you have chosen and become familiar with local laws and zoning that affect restaurants.
- Look into all aspects of acquiring a specific site for your business, including the possibility of purchasing an existing restaurant, or the lease or purchase of a suitable building.

You must accept the fact that, unless you are already a well-known personality, location is more important than any other single factor in your future success. Is another new restaurant really needed at the place you have tentatively selected? The answer will depend on whom you ask; but one way to find out is to go and stay there for a few days yourself to try out the local eating places. If you have no trouble obtaining several really good meals in more than one place, and if they are reasonably priced, maybe your itch to open your very own place can best be scratched by taking over one of the good restaurants you visited. You will find a discussion of purchasing an existing restaurant in Chapter 3.

Where should you open? Selecting a location while you are working full-time can be difficult unless you live in the vicinity or you can adjust your working schedule. It can take many months or even years to find the right spot to open your business, but this effort will pay off.

Narrow down your intended clientele to suit your particular forte in cooking, and you will have established a principal determining factor in site selection. For example, you may make fantastic omelets, but are you really interested in breakfast and lunch as a specialty? If so, you can choose from several possible locations where people eat those meals in sufficient numbers for you to make a business of it. A central business district ("CBD" in planners' terms) of any reasonable-size community offers one choice. Or, if a small town is your goal, the likelihood of picking up transient business may be the difference between economic success and failure. Does the town have a lot of traffic passing nearby, or is it in a resort area where you can pick up referrals from motels? Is there a main thoroughfare or highway with access to a potential restaurant site? Do tourists visit the area because of some nearby attraction, such as a natural area of great beauty or a recreational facility?

Talk to area planners. Check with the local planning officials, such as the city or county planning director and the local chamber of commerce. You should learn something of interest. But always verify the reported status of planned growth by consulting other sources of information. If a new industry is expected to locate in the town, the public relations department of the company should be willing to discuss timetables with you for a few minutes, if the plans are firm. Real estate people and chamber of commerce spokesmen tend to exaggerate schedules. They often play down or fail to mention uncertainties and known delays. But you will be able to discover them if you do your homework well.

Finally, remember that everyone with whom you talk in your chosen area is a potential customer of your restaurant. So look good when you call on them in person, and be as pleasant and cooperative as possible, even if they are not. Their impression of you may be critical to your first year's success.

ZONING AND OTHER LOCAL REGULATIONS

When you visit the planning department, obtain copies of the following regulations and ordinances, as well as other useful facts:

1. Zoning laws which specify the districts in which your planned type of restaurant is permitted.
2. Procedure for obtaining a conditional use permit and/or zoning variance, if one is required.
3. Parking requirements for restaurants.
4. On-site and off-site sign regulations.
5. The names of each of the official planning board members or commissioners, and of the planning director.
6. The names of the councilmen, supervisors, aldermen, select-men (or however the local politicos are designated) who serve the district in which you are planning to operate.
7. The most recent regional planning document for the locale.
8. The name of the local non-official citizens advisory planning group, if any, and the name and phone number of its chairman or president.
9. The names of any local "concerned citizens council" or other community pressure group that might influence your case, should you have any reason to need their support or neutral-

ize their opposition to your plans. You are most likely to need their help if you are planning a new building or an extensive remodeling of an existing building, especially if you are going to make some wonderful old home into a restaurant.

Restaurant red tape. If your plan is to reopen a restaurant site that had been an operating establishment in the past, that will not exempt you from all the planning and building department red tape. The most logical time for new regulations to be imposed on an old location, after all, is when there is a new owner or operator of the old wreck. The most common form of enforcement of these regulations is the withholding of needed permits, licenses, certificates, and the like until you comply with or obtain a waiver of the requirements. New statutes are coming thick and fast these days to solve problems in sewage disposal (restaurant grease is a big problem), water conservation (restaurants waste a lot), access for the elderly and the handicapped, visual and noise pollution (signs for "fast food" places are an outrage), and on-street parking congestion near residential neighborhoods (if you are a huge success, it could happen!); and to meet requirements for smoking and nonsmoking sections, Occupational Safety and Health Act (OSHA) standards, and other rules you would not in your wildest dreams imagine could apply to your little place of business.

Even if you don't have a building site tied down yet, do not be put off by the government clerk to whom you direct your request for the information you need. If he tells you to come back when you can pinpoint the block on which you intend to be, at least ask to see the key pages of the applicable ordinances and read them, making appropriate notes. Be persistent, as well as pleasant and patient. You might have to remind him tactfully that he is there to serve the very purposes for which you ask his assistance.

Commercial building requirements. Be sure to pay a visit to the building inspection department too, if it is not a part of the planning office. At least get the name of the chief inspector, if you plan on having any work done that will require a building permit. Later, when you decide on a specific site and a final design, pay visits to the key people in a timely manner. It can't hurt, and it might even help, if you are especially beautiful or charming.

Some of the safety requirements for public buildings such as restaurants are useful and reasonable. But others are not really essential. Do you hate concrete? The county engineer (retired last year from the Army Corps of Engineers) who issues your remodeling permit doesn't hate concrete. He loves concrete curbs, gutters, and sidewalks, and you should see his ordinance. Armed with it, he can shoot down your dreams with a requirement for a ten-foot sidewalk as well as a concrete curb and gutter in front of your little place, at a cost of $25 per linear foot for everything.

Let's say you have a lot in the shape of a trapezoid with 250 feet of frontage on Main Street and only 95 feet on the back alley. The county engineer may "help" you by agreeing that it won't be necessary to install curb, gutter, and sidewalk along the alley—just along the Main Street frontage. (Twenty-five dollars times 250 feet equals $6,250.) So, before he issues the remodeling permit for your restaurant, he will insist on your making a $6,250 deposit with the county treasurer as a completion bond. He will demand that you sign an agreement to install the curb, gutter, and sidewalk in compliance with his engineered plans. Of course, the county will give you six months to do it.

What if you don't get it done in six months? Why, then it will be done for you by county workers, and if the $6,250 doesn't cover it, you'll be billed for the difference. That's why he will urge you to do it right away. Costs are going up all the time.

Poof! There goes your remodeling budget. Did you think that the $6,250 should be spent for a walk-in refrigerator and freezer? You're right. But then again maybe you were never in the Army Corps of Engineers. The only way out of this kind of problem is to get a waiver of the requirement. Don't be discouraged; just be prepared.

REAL ESTATE CONSIDERATIONS

Lease or purchase? Do you have a sensible friend in the real estate field who will help you find the property you want? If not, seek out a broker with a reputation for reliability. Here are some of the questions you will want answered by a real estate agent who shows commercial property. These questions should cover both lease and outright purchase of the site.

For *leasing,* you should find out about:

- Long-term availability and renewal options.
- Condition of the building and whether it meets all current codes—electrical (including availability of 220-volt power), water, gas, and sewage service.
- Fire rating for insurance purposes, and insurance responsibility.
- Maintenance and repair responsibility.
- Services available for garbage and trash removal, snow removal, and gardening.
- Off-street parking facilities.
- Permitted uses for the zoning category, including any existing variances or conditional uses allowed only by permit.
- Agreements or lease restrictions covering use of the building or adjacent businesses.
- Past restrictions on the licenses of previous tenants.

For a building that you are considering *purchasing,* in addition to the above you should know:

- Assessed valuation and taxes on the land and improvements.
- Deed restrictions.
- Existing loans and payoff; whether you can assume the loan, and at what interest rate.
- Other outstanding liens against the property.
- Structural pest condition.
- Existence of any conditional use permits and if they are renewable when the property changes ownership.
- Any equipment, fixtures, and plants, if included with the building.

Formulate the questions in your own words and practice answering questions that the agents will ask. Your answers will establish in the agent's mind your qualifications as a buyer or lessee. Prepare a written summary of your needs and desires, your budget (how much cash you can beg, borrow, or steal), your timetable, and your expectations. You can always change the list or make compromises, but preparing it will save you time.

Remodeling. As a general rule it doesn't pay to make a major investment in remodeling a building you do not own. If your budget makes it impossible for you to open in your own building, do not plan on extensive remodeling unless the landlord is willing to share in the cost. (This is unlikely.) If you do spend a bundle on redecorating or remodeling, secure the assurance, by means of a reasonably long-term lease, that your rent will not be raised for the first two or three critical years. If you go ahead with substantial improvements to the building, especially to the outside, its assessed valuation is bound to increase. Shortly thereafter, the landlord's tax bill will go up accordingly. (Every building permit that is issued causes an indicator to be set in the tax assessors' computer, which then prints out "Inspect and Reassess.") The landlord will then repay your efforts to improve his property by raising your rent, using the justification that his taxes have gone up. You must negotiate some equitable consideration for any expenditures you make on his building.

Evaluating rentals. If you are not able to buy your site, an important part of your groundwork is to evaluate the kinds of leases available in the area. Start by asking the landlord of an existing restaurant what are the terms of the lease, giving the reason you want to know. He may refuse to divulge that information, but what do you have to lose by asking? You can always check with the restaurant owner to verify what he tells you. Another source for such data is a local real estate broker who specializes in commercial property, or even a restaurant broker.

The monthly rent specified in a lease may be tied to the gross income of the business, or to the equipment provided by the lessor, or it may vary by month in seasonal locations. But you need an idea of the general run of rents in the area; you can then compare them based on dining-room square footage, number of tables and seats (including counter seats), and the other factors directly related to the production of income. It is also important to apportion correctly the monthly rent of a site where the restaurant operation is combined with another activity such as a bakery, a bar that serves liquor, a store, or any business not directly involving food service.

Be cautious when you ask questions, the better to determine how trustworthy your lessor or agent is. Learn to ask probing questions in a friendly manner. Try to ask a key question several times, phrased in different ways, at different points in the conversation to see if you will get consistent answers. Take someone else with you who has knowledge in a related area of any sort. This person should just listen and occasionally ask a question to help clarify what you are told. When you have completed your interview, prepare notes immediately in the car or at a coffee shop, to be sure you have a complete record of what was said. A month later when you actually go to negotiate a lease, those notes may be invaluable if the story has been changed. Your friend who listened to the answers and helped to make accurate notes can serve as a witness.

Buying time with an option. If you have the capital, do not hesitate to use the "option" method for tying up a possible location for a short time. It is possible to purchase the exclusive right, for a week or a month or more, to buy or lease a piece of property. Such an option could cost you anywhere from $500 to $5,000 or more, but it might buy you the time needed to choose between two properties which are not both available at the same time. However, you must complete all the hard bargaining on the price of the eventual purchase or lease, plus all conditions and terms, *before* you sign an option, so that such terms are made a part of the option agreement. Of course, you must be willing to forfeit the cost of the option in the event that you choose not to exercise it. But in certain circumstances it might be worth it just to have the time to decide carefully. And the option cost should always be applicable to the sale price or first month's rent if you do exercise the option.

Do not use the option method if you are simply undecided about what to do; use it when you have two good choices of property whose status cannot be determined simultaneously. An option on the first one will hold it. Sometimes a simple offer with a substantial deposit and appropriate approval (escape) clauses can serve just as well to tie up the property; but this will not give you an exclusive right to buy it, unless you have offered the asking price and met all of the seller's conditions. Thus, your offer may allow the owner to take ten days to decide, but it is still his option, not yours, to accept or reject or make a counter-offer. If you need more like thirty days, or perhaps several months, to make a decision, you might buy the time.

Consider the time of year when you make an option offer. For example, if a property for sale or lease is in a summer resort community and you are aiming for a May opening, it might pay in October or November to negotiate a ninety-day option to purchase.

The likelihood that the property would be sold during those months is smaller, so you should be able to buy the option for a lower cost. This will still allow the seller to advertise and move the property in the spring, should you fail to reach agreement.

Finally, the specific terms of your option agreement should be reviewed beforehand by your real estate broker friend and your lawyer.

If you are locating in a town that has any sort of special heritage or historic significance, consider it a signal advantage. Do the research necessary to learn the local history and anecdotes. You will have ample opportunity to make dining at your place even more memorable for visitors by relating a good story at appropriate moments.

DON'T FORGET ABOUT THE FOOD

If all this groundwork leaves you with any spare time, or if you have children whom you want to involve in the process, there is one more task. All these years you must have been mulling over the sorts of meals you would serve in your own restaurant. Well, it is time to stop mulling and to begin accumulating recipes—for large groups, and for small groups, too. Since most home cookbooks are designed for relatively small numbers of diners, you can do some conversion by multiplying quantities of ingredients and sizes of pots and pans. The conversion method of extrapolating some recipes is a good exercise to give a child learning arithmetic and fractions, and can be a practical means of family participation in the effort to establish the restaurant. But it is also useful to find out how many people can be served from, say, ten or twenty quarts of a dish. These figures are available from cookbooks written for serving large groups.

Unless you possess total recall, you should begin a file of recipes that you will use, including your own secret ones. You can't begin too soon to collect, test, and revise interesting recipes to suit your taste. An acceptable recipe is one that is good enough to be worth the labor involved in preparation. There are all sorts of marvelous dishes on which you are not likely to make any money, because few people will pay you for the time necessary to prepare them. Either stay away from these dishes or find shortcuts. Serving time and convenience for the chef and servers are other factors to consider in planning some types of entrees. Too many side dishes make serving a chore on a busy night.

This book is not intended as a recipe book, however, either for cooking or for opening a restaurant. There are no proven recipes for the latter—only experience, good sense, and an inherent feeling for what pleases the public with style.

Many excellent restaurateurs prepared for their careers by catering for large parties of friends and acquaintances.

---

3.   Actually Doing It

YOU have now found the spot where you will establish your restaurant. You have decided what kind of food you will serve. You have become a regular at the restaurant equipment auctions and you have a good idea of the kind and cost of the equipment available. What happens next?

START WITH THE HEALTH DEPARTMENT

The first person you should see is the local health inspector or sanitarian, who should know all the restaurants in the area, as well as all the regulations for them. Come away from your first visit to him or her with a copy of the restaurant act or food service sanitary code for your state, and a copy of the checklist used by the inspector in the final inspection of a restaurant before a health permit to operate is issued. Study these documents well, and prepare to comply. Upon preliminary inspection of your selected site and building, a reasonable health inspector may tell you which items on the list you must fully comply with before the final inspection, and which items he may give you some leeway time on.

There was not one regulation in the California Restaurant Act, which was our guide, that did not make sense; nor was the county set of regulations, which was sometimes more stringent than the state's, unreasonable in any instance. Be sure you understand the requirements, both as written and as *interpreted* by the local inspector.

If you have chosen a building for your restaurant that is the site of a former eatery, examine the record of past health inspections at that location. You may learn something of value in your negotiations with the landlord or owner. If you have not yet made up your mind about a place, but are close to making a deal, ask the health inspector to look at it and advise you how much you must do to comply with current regulations. This information is essential, and it should be free, if you are willing to arrange the visit at the inspector's convenience. Even if you intend to build a new structure or to add to an existing one, you and your architect should have advance information on what the inspector will require.

The plans for your building or remodeling will have to be reviewed by the health department. There may be certain special items, however, such as the need for a sewer line grease interceptor (or grease trap), which the building or sewer department rather than the health department has the responsibility to approve. The health department review will be primarily concerned with the kitchen, storage areas, dishwashing facility, maintenance facility, and public and employee rest rooms. This department's interest in the dining room will be generally limited to the server station, salad bar, or beverage bar—that is, any place where food or drink is stored or dispensed outside the kitchen.

You will design your kitchen to suit your menu; and you should have decided upon your probable menu before you visit the health department. The inspector will want an idea of the meals you intend to serve, and an understanding of the extent of your menu for all the mealtimes you plan to be open. Why? He will determine the type and capacity of refrigeration you must have to maintain wholesomeness from day to day. The more ambitious the menu, the more refrigerated storage space you will be expected to have.

INSURANCE CONSIDERATIONS

Fire insurance. Insurability is an important part of the protection of your investment. In searching for a site, one important factor to be aware of is the fire rating for the location; this is given on a scale of one to ten, with one being the best rating. Any fire insurance under-writer or competent insurance broker can obtain the rating for a specific location, which is dependent on such factors as the quality of water pressure, the type of fire department serving the area and its training status, and the quality and amount of local firefighting equipment.

Your fire insurance premium will depend on a number of things, including, but not limited to, the fire district rating, the rating of your building type, the kind of equipment in the kitchen (deep fat fryers cost you), the type of fire extinguishing equipment you have, and your experience in the restaurant business. Does this last item surprise you? Ponder this: of all the restaurants that fail during their first year of operation, 70 percent burn down. Some undoubtedly fail because they accidentally burn. But many would not have "accidentally" burned if they had not been failing. Moral: you won't go to jail for burning the steak, but you certainly will get into a lot of hot water if it burns after closing time.

Liquor liability. One of the more expensive forms of insurance coverage in recent years has been that for "liquor liability," especially for hard liquor. This kind of insurance protects you in suits filed by third parties for damages or injuries caused by your imbibing patrons. There has been an alarming increase recently in the amount of damages awarded by juries in such cases. The injury does not have to take place in your establishment for you to be held responsible in many jurisdictions; the drinker can leave your place and get into an accident later, and if he is underinsured you may well find yourself in court. Liquor liability insurance is therefore essential.

This point is a good one at which to interject a few comments on the serving of distilled spirits in your little restaurant. Fermented spirits—beer, wine, champagne, fortified wines, and sherries—are a wonderful complement to any menu. They aid digestion, relaxation, and general well-being. They can be joyous and elegant libations, in moderation. I heartily recommend wine with any meal, especially in cities where the water is polluted or is a liquid carcinogen. But, whenever distilled spirits—hard liquor—are served as an adjunct to dining, especially in larger restaurants with big overhead costs, there is an inherent danger of the emphasis shifting away from good food service toward higher liquor consumption. (Have you ever been kept at the bar until you finished two or three rounds, only to discover a half-empty dining room when you were finally allowed to have your table?) The higher percentage of profit on liquor is too attractive to management, particularly where a distilled spirits license for on-premises consumption is a large investment. In certain counties in California, for instance, restaurateurs have paid more than $75,000 for a general liquor license alone, not including the premises. Such an expenditure demands that the owner push liquor sales to recoup his investment at an equitable rate.

In my experience, the food and service in restaurants that have bars have rarely been excellent. For a small restaurant, unless the initial cost of the license is very low (say, under $15,000), it is my opinion that alcoholic beverage service is best limited to fermented spirits. Heavy consumption of alcohol in any form dulls the palate, dims the eyes, and often fouls the aroma and shatters the mood of a fine dining room. For those who enjoy an after-dinner liqueur, it is better to find a nice cozy bar to adjourn to after leaving the restaurant, or, best of all, to be invited home to enjoy such libations.

More discussion of other forms of liability is included in Chapter 12.

WHAT SHOULD YOU BUDGET FOR DECOR?

Put fresh flowers on the table; and avoid gaudy table candles, menu "tents" that stand on the table, and the other gimcracks that abound in a thousand coffee shops.

Millions of dollars are being spent in "theme" restaurants all over the country to give the illusion of long-lost images of Casablanca, robber barons' private railroad cars, Eddie Rickenbacker's orderly room, King Solomon's mines, *ad nauseam*. These fantastic sums spent in creating a theme do not influence by one iota the quality of the food that is served. They merely attempt to delude your perception of the quality. It is the food itself that counts; everything else supplements and complements the main effort. Comfortable chairs, pleasing table settings, crisp linen, interesting dishware and glassware all contribute something. But these accessories will never disguise stale, tepid, or otherwise unappetizing food, nor compensate for unconcerned service.

Simplicity and a feeling of cleanliness are more important than unique and wonderful things on the walls. I do not pretend to be a decorator. My observations are based on comments from thousands of customers, many of whom have mentioned simplicity and cleanliness as contributing to their dining pleasure. Budget accordingly.

PLANNING DINING ROOM CAPACITY

How many tables will you have in your dining room? The architect will come up with one number, to comply with safety and fire regulations, and to provide enough chair and aisle space. Even if you find ways of squeezing in more on busy nights, you must maintain safe access for customers and servers, as well as the minimum comfortable social distance for privacy. You must also consider your flexibility in handling the typical mix of parties, ranging from the single diner to groups of ten or more, with the majority being "deuces," "fours," and "sixes." For example, it is impractical in a small restaurant to have only round tables, because you cannot easily push two or three together to serve parties of eight, ten, twelve, or more. This may not be a problem to you; perhaps you prefer not to accommodate such parties, or perhaps you have a separate room for large groups. But why restrict your dining room capacity and flexibility?

There are other considerations in establishing an "official capacity." Insurance rates may be tied to this number, as may other things including the number of required rest rooms, the monthly sewer service fee, the commercial water rate per unit, the need for smoking and nonsmoking sections in the room, and the number of fire exits. The typical limit, above which you must comply with stricter requirements, is fifty diners. The number of off-street parking spaces required is also likely to be tied to the number of tables and employees.

The fire marshal in your area will be interested in your kitchen protection against fire, and also in other aspects of fire safety for the entire building. He will prescribe the number of fire exits, maximum capacity for the dining room, use of fire walls, and requirements in other areas of his expertise. He will want all doors from the dining room to open out, and to have locks that cannot be accidentally locked during business hours.

OFF-STREET PARKING

Your parking lot can be a headache, but it is a necessary one in most communities. If the lot is to serve you well, it should be adequately lighted at night and properly identified for use by your patrons. Do not overlook the possibility of arranging for additional nighttime parking at a nearby bank building, or at any other business lot otherwise in use only during the daytime. You can always require your staff to park outside your lot so as to reserve more space for customers; but remember that parking lots that are secluded and poorly lighted are unsafe for waitresses carrying home their tips late at night or owners carrying the day's receipts. (If you can arrange for it, a big safe or a built-in floor or wall safe is a good idea, for extra cash and the night's receipts.)

REMODELING A BUILDING

Even if you select a former restaurant site, you may decide to do extensive remodeling. And some of the loveliest restaurants are in buildings previously used for utterly different purposes.

Building contractors. The selection of a contractor to do your building or remodeling is not a simple matter of looking in the yellow pages, obtaining bids, and picking the lowest bidder. If possible, you should choose a contractor who has already built at least one restaurant in the area, or perhaps has worked on a small hospital or other facility whose operation must be inspected by the health department. Such a contractor will be more likely to do the job to the satisfaction of the health inspector. If you can afford a managing or supervising architect who will monitor the work, it is possible that the aggravation you will be spared justifies the extra expense. It depends on how much you know, how much time you have to devote to the project, and what you can afford to pay others to do for you.

Power requirements for a restaurant. The electrical service for the building is crucial to your plan for equipment. For certain electric motors you must have single-phase 220-volt service. Your dishwashing machine is likely to require 220 volts, and items such as toasters and exhaust fan motors are available in either 110V or 220V versions. The 220V equipment is more economical than 110V to operate, but sometimes more expensive to buy. Be certain that 220V service is available in the building, and plan for convenient power outlets in the kitchen. In general, you can never have too many 110V outlets in a restaurant kitchen.

You may find that your small town does not have three-phase 220V electrical service available in all parts of town and that therefore your forty-quart Hobart mixer with all attachments (on which you got such a wonderful bargain) is now a big white elephant because it operates only on three-phase 220V power.

If you are fortunate enough to find an existing restaurant building to take over, many of the concerns listed above will have already been resolved, but you should be knowledgeable about them anyway. Always try to obtain a complete wiring diagram for the building showing where the conduit is in the walls. (The same is true for water, drain, and gas lines.) The circuit breaker panel should be properly labeled to allow quick isolation of the cause of interruptions in electrical service.

Ventilation. Proper ventilation is imperative for a small restaurant. Patron and staff comfort depends on your ability to regulate the temperature and amount of smoke in the dining room. Grease-laden hot air over the kitchen range and griddle, hot air over the ovens, and steam and vapor over the dishwashing machine and steam table must be exhausted. If you fail to provide a sufficient volume of replacement air to the kitchen, you may discover that smoke produced in the dining room by gourmet nicotine freaks will be drawn into the kitchen, where it fouls the chef's olfactory and gustatory senses. Heaven forbid.

We had a worse problem. We established a small restaurant in an old home, and our dining room boasted a lovely little fireplace. The first time we tried to burn wood in it at dinnertime, the dining room quickly filled up with dense smoke. It seems that the hood fan in the kitchen counteracted the natural draft of the fireplace chimney so that air was being drawn down the chimney instead of up. To permit use of the old fireplace, a special exhaust system had to be designed and installed—with a concomitant increase in the electric bill. Almost any ventilation problem can be solved with money and time—two scarce commodities at any small restaurant.

Windows in the dining room. A few other aspects of your potential restaurant building are of more than passing interest. If you have the choice of designing your dining room with or without windows, put them in, unless the view outside is absolutely distasteful. Don't worry that if you have only a few window tables patrons who cannot have one will be unhappy. The customer always has the option to reserve a window table or to wait for one. (Besides, the food is the same at any table.)

If your place in on the ground level, it is nice for potential customers to be able to look inside through a window, or to see diners sitting at table by the window. And there is something special about sitting at a window while eating, and watching the world go by. It is a compensation the world allows for people who have to, or choose to, eat alone. A window also affords you a decorating opportunity to make your place look more attractive from the outside or more interesting from the inside. Real flowers, even in a window box, are associated with fine dining in the minds of many people, including me.

The American public is loath to walk out of a restaurant once they have entered. They will not go into the place just to check it out. If you want people to come inside because you think they will like it, post your menu on a window where they can see the inside as well.

Windows in the kitchen. Windows in the kitchen are another story. They can let in light and air, but they may also admit flies in the summer through holes in the screens. The windows also present a security problem if they open to a secluded spot such as an alley; and this is a factor to contend with when you have valuable equipment or decor. You can have bars put on the rear windows, but it is expensive. Finally, if the kitchen windows look out to a reasonably pleasant scene and allow observation of the rear of the building, they will be appreciated by the kitchen staff. Unnecessary windows can always be boarded up, or solid walls can be opened with small fixed glass openings, if needed, to afford some view.

Plan for enough refrigerated storage. Storage space, or the lack of it, is a major drawback is most restaurant buildings. The presence of a conveniently placed walk-in cooler and freezer makes a tremendous difference in the operation and profitability of a restaurant. Refrigeration units are designated "reach-in" or "walk-in" to differentiate their size and function. The walk-in provides a larger capacity, primarily for storage of supplies between meals and between deliveries, as well as for replenishment of the working refrigerators during busy times. The reach-in box is intended as a strategically placed unit to hold ingredients and raw foods during actual food preparation. It must be immediately accessible to the chef and his assistants. The design of the kitchen is so crucial to successful operation that the entire next chapter is devoted to the subject.

Schedule delays in construction. Your projected schedule from the start of construction or of remodeling to opening day should have a large margin of slack time in it to allow for unforeseen delays. Some have already been alluded to, such as the necessity for you to post a performance bond or meet other local regulations before a building permit will be issued. Your contractor may anticipate some delays in his estimate, or he may not be willing to predict a completion date at all, but in your own mind you should avoid wishful thinking and add at least 25 percent to the scheduled construction time. In other words, if you hope to open to the public four months after you secure your location, plan for a likely opening in five or six months. If you cannot afford such a delay, your plans may be too ambitious for your budget.

BUYING YOUR DREAM (OR SOMEONE ELSE'S)

If you feel that all the trouble you may have to go through in building or remodeling before you even serve one meal is not worth it, there is another option to consider. You can buy an existing restaurant and take over its operation, reserving changes for the future if that seems more sensible. It is certainly a possibility worth pursuing seriously. Your stomach lining may appreciate it. Buying an operating restaurant offers you the advantage of immediate income, an established reputation and clientele, and the chance to see exactly what you are buying before you invest much money.

The disadvantages are equally compelling, but they vary according to whether you want to buy a successful restaurant or one in which the owner/operator is in some distress. That distress may be unrelated to the condition of the business. The owner may be dissolving a marriage, for instance, or may be seriously ill, or may have suffered the loss of a partner or family member who was essential to the business.

Purchase price. If you want to buy a successful restaurant, be prepared to pay a high price. The more cash you can put down, the better the deal you can make. If the building is not part of the sale, you can expect to invest less money, but the terms and duration of the lease are very important to the feasibility of the transaction.

The tangible assets of the business include the equipment, fixtures, and furnishings, plus the stock and leasehold. The intangible assets, such as the location and the restaurant's name and reputation, are much more difficult to evaluate. The records of gross income and profits in prior years are one indicator, though there is never any guarantee that these will hold true under new management. This portion of the sale price is therefore sometimes called the "blue sky" part.

If the building is part of the deal, you will analyze that factor just as if you were establishing your place from scratch. Here you have an advantage, for you can easily compare the value of the real property with other commercial property in the area. The real property portion of the deal may also allow you to work out a better split between the cash down payment and the secured debt portion of the sale price.

One of your main considerations in making an offer will be your projected ability to recoup the cash investment in full within a certain number of years. Your risk of not being able to retire the debt incurred in the purchase depends on the income and expense figures that are verifiable, and on your cash reserve for contingencies. You do not want to end up paying all your profits to the former owner for many years. One thing to consider where the debt portion of the sale price is secured by negotiable paper (notes, trust deeds, or mortgages) is this: if the holder of the paper decides later to sell it to someone at a discount, you should reserve the right to first refusal of the deal. That is, if you sign a note to secure a debt of $10,000, which the holder is willing to sell later at a 25 percent discount, you might find a way to come up with $7,500 in cash from another source and thus save $2,500.

Verification of assets. To verify what you are buying you must have access to the restaurant's books, bank records, and invoices. You will also want to verify the *net spendable income* for prior years by seeing the pertinent portions of the current owners' income tax returns. (It may pay you to hire a certified public accountant to assist you in the analysis.) Before you will be allowed such access, you will have to establish yourself as a principal—that is, a serious, financially qualified buyer. The usual way to do this is by depositing a substantial amount of "earnest money"—perhaps five to ten thousand dollars. It can be arranged that your deposit will be refunded if the books are not to your satisfaction.

Your ability to observe and to ask questions will assist you in deciding whether to pursue the deal aggressively. You should plan to observe the business operation for a few days, especially during the peak hours, but also on slack days. You should pose these specific questions to the owner:

- How many meals of each type are served each week, and how do these numbers vary with the season?
- What is the monthly payroll? Does it include the owners' salary or draw?
- What percentage of gross sales is represented by food? By alcoholic beverages? By any other sales?
- What is the breakdown of various business expenses—cost of sales, employee wages and benefits, overhead and other fixed expenses—expressed as a percentage of gross income?
- How much was spent last year on maintenance and repair?
- How much was spent last year on capital improvements and equipment? What was purchased?
- Who are the main suppliers for dairy products, produce, fish, meat, staples, and alcoholic beverages?

You should ask for a complete inventory of the equipment, fixtures, and furniture included in the sale price. You should expect to have the option to purchase the existing stock of food and beverages at or below cost, but this is not likely to be included in the sale price. The only instance in which it actually makes a big difference in the amount of cash necessary to buy the place is when there is an extensive and valuable stock of wine. Remember, any transfer of ownership of alcoholic beverages is subject to the approval of the alcoholic beverage control commission.

Most small restaurants do not employ certified public accountants. If one has been used, however, the C.P.A.'s statements of financial condition and profit and loss in prior years, as well as current year-to-date figures, should be of great value in the initial evaluation of the deal.

Once you have answers to your questions and you have a

verified figure for gross sales and projected sales for the current year based on year-to-date figures, you can then use the number of meals served to determine what the average customer spends for a meal at this restaurant. You might also plan to make some changes in the hours of operation that would allow you to increase volume without too much increase in labor costs. Basically, you are interested in whatever slack exists in the current operation's attempt to realize its full potential for income. This slack may be in the form of too-low prices, inefficient use of labor, too large a menu resulting in waste, or operating hours that ignore a significant number of customers. If the restaurant is successful, of course, there is less chance that significant slack exists.

Reputation and recipes. When you know who the suppliers are, you should arrange to discuss the restaurant with the salespeople and perhaps also the district manager of the key suppliers. As a potential customer, you are likely to be treated with respect, though they will probably not discuss any problems that they might be held liable for revealing to you. If you can establish your credentials and a good rapport, you may get some valuable negotiating information, especially if the operation is in any serious financial trouble. Another source of information can be local businesspeople who know the restaurant. Also talk with the bank manager where the restaurant's business account is held. Discretion will limit the information you can obtain, but if the reputation is good you will get positive indications from these sources.

One of the tangible assets of a highly successful restaurant with a unique menu may well be the recipes of the chef or owner. Try to get possession of these as part of the purchase agreement, but it is unlikely that you will readily or cheaply obtain them. (It might pay for you to eat a lot of meals at the place before you reveal yourself as a serious buyer, just so you will have a basis for comparing recipes later.)

Noncompetition agreements. It is also very important to find out whether the chef or owner intends to pursue the same career in the area after you buy the restaurant. To protect yourself and your investment, you must extract a noncompetition agreement from the seller. Even a seriously ill chef can recover in a few months. A retired chef may decide to return to the field part-time at another place in the same town. If you have paid a high price for the exclusive right to a well-known name and reputation, and for the recipes to continue a popular menu, then you have a right to exclude the originator from competing with you in the surrounding area for a period of at least five years. The actual radius for a small restaurant might be as little as ten miles or as much as several hundred, if it is famous and expensive enough. A good business lawyer with experience in the field can assist you in preparing a binding agreement. It will normally proscribe the sellers from owning or operating a competing food service establishment of any sort that caters to the general public. It probably cannot prevent them, however, from working for a salary in a place where they have no management responsibility or ownership interest.

If you do some innovative things with your restaurant that prove successful, expect to see your ideas "borrowed" by others. It's a free country. If they do it as well as you do, the public is better served. If they do not, you still have your reputation intact. If they do it even better, get on the ball and outdo them all again.

YOUR MENU

A menu serves two purposes. First, it is a communication direct from the chef to the diner. Besides listing the items offered, it often describes briefly how the dish is prepared and served. Second, the menu serves as the most basic form of advertising. Many dinner patrons will not be aware, for example, that you serve a Sunday brunch or a daily luncheon; your menu should announce the availability of other meal service. Also on the menu should appear your name, your hours of service, your location, the ownership, and the type of food you consider your specialty. A surprisingly large number of patrons will request a souvenir menu or one to show their friends. Many are happy to purchase one at a nominal charge.

Menu design and layout is really a matter of common sense, legibility, and simple arithmetic. Few small restaurants have need for large or elaborate menus. I favor separate menus for each mealtime served; but at dinner, I strongly favor using a limited menu with the main offerings listed on a blackboard or on a separate sheet that can be prepared daily. If you use a standard printed menu, you can still list daily "specials" on a blackboard, or have the server mention them at the table. The menu that varies daily offers tremendous flexibility for taking advantage of special food bargains, and avoids the spoilage problems inherent in maintaining a larger, fixed bill of fare. More is said about the use of blackboard menus later in this chapter.

The most prominent message at the top of your menu should be the name of the mealtime—breakfast, lunch, dinner, or whatever. The days and hours of service are an important corollary. Depending on how extensive your bill of fare is, you may wish to group the offerings into salads, sandwiches, appetizers, special items, hot meals, side dishes, desserts, and beverages. Any supplemental information about items on the menu should be placed so that it does not interfere with a quick scan of all the offerings.

Dinner patrons, because they have more time to order and eat, tend to want more description of how each dish is prepared and served. The main items on a printed dinner menu should be followed by simple, appetizing descriptions of the cut of meat, fish, or fowl offered, and of the accompanying sauce or stuffing, if any. Do use well-known names for popular entrees, even if you make them in your own special style; fancy new names just confuse the customer. Be accurate in your choice of descriptive terms, listing specific ingredients where appropriate, and be certain to mention if any dishes are highly seasoned or spiced. But don't go into paroxysms of detail or praise. Often the menu description sounds better than the food actually tastes when it arrives. Your menu should pass this test: is the information useful to the customer?

Make price comparison easy by listing the price of each item in a prominent position. I favor listing items in ascending order of costliness, with the least expensive first. But it is not necessary to have a strict order, just a trend from lower to higher prices.

The chef and servers will always develop a shorthand code for handling orders. Some coffee shops assign a number to each menu item; but this makes deletions from and additions to the menu difficult.

It is best not to clutter up your menu with a lot of little low-priced side orders. People will ask for them whether they are listed on the menu or not. If you find that a few are always requested, add them to the next revision of the menu to save the servers time.

THE
BOGUS RESTAURANT

Uptown Center
Someplace, Pennsyltucky

DINNER

Served from 5 p.m. to 10 p.m. daily
Closed Mondays

Appetizers

Fresh Melon with Lime	$1.50
Marinated Artichoke Hearts	1.75
Herring in Wine Sauce	2.00
Skewered Chicken Liver and Water Chestnut Wrapped in Bacon and Broiled	2.95

Soups

Prepared daily in our kitchen $1.95

Hearty Vegetable

French Onion with Imported Swiss Cheese

Vichyssoise

Gazpacho

Fresh Clam Chowder (Fridays only)

Beverages

Fresh-ground coffee	$1.00
Our special coffee	1.25
Selection of teas, per pot	1.00
Espresso, a pot for two	1.95
The Dinner Sundae— Vanilla or coffee ice cream, our homemade hot fudge sauce, fresh whipped cream, and nuts.	2.50

Entrees

All dinners served with house appetizer, garden salad, baked potato or cottage fries or rice, and a choice of fresh vegetable. For a la carte, subtract $1.50.

Fresh Catch of the Day—The local yield from Lake Bogus, stream, or sea, priced accordingly.

Cashew Chicken—Tender chunks of light and dark chicken with snow peas, sprouts, cashew nuts, and bamboo shoots in a tangy sauce; served with rice ... $9.50

Chef's Choice—A special dinner announced each evening, which reflects the chef's skill to please your palate with the best available meat, fish, or fowl. ... 10.95

Rib Eye Steak—12 to 14 ounces of aged beef, prepared to your order. ... 12.95

Lamb Kebobs—Choice chunks of spring lamb skewered with fresh green pepper and onion in a special marinade of Middle Eastern origin, on a bed of rice pilaf. ... 12.95

Desserts

Orange or Lime Sherbet ... $1.25

Homemade Pastries from our Cart, individually priced

New York Cheesecake (enough for two) ... 2.00

Fresh Fruit with Imported Gruyere Cheese ... 3.25

Reservations accepted   Call 555-4444

Menu graphics. Unless you are artistically talented and can do it yourself, hire a graphic artist to prepare a basic border and cover design for your menu, to provide an attractive setting for the written material. You will want to explore with the designer your alternatives for paper, colors, printing, and the like. Once the master for this design is created, it should be saved for repeated use when your menu changes. It is wise to have several photostats made of the original artwork, in case it gets lost or defaced.

Whether typewritten, typeset, or hand-lettered, your menu lettering should be of medium size (approximately twelve-point to sixteen-point type) for maximum legibility. The main items should be in larger or bolder type or lettering; and prices should be placed so they are easy to read and to compare. Before your menu actually goes to press, read the final master carefully to eliminate errors in prices and descriptions of dishes.

Blackboard menus. I use the term "blackboard" to mean any easily altered form of menu that announces to entering patrons and to each table the fare for that mealtime. It may take the form of an actual chalkboard on the wall or on an easel that can be readily moved from table to table. But it just as well can be a piece of white, or light-colored, smooth-surfaced material on which crayon, grease pencil, or glass marker can be used to write the menu. (The appropriate solvent for erasure and alteration is necessary.)

The use of an actual black or green chalkboard does not mean that it must be inelegant or sloppy. Even the most excellent dining room will accept such a board framed in beautifully carved hardwood or decorated with some kind of lovely border design.

The key to successful use of a blackboard menu is in its legibility, its availability to the diners at the time they need to refer to it, and the ease with which the management can alter or delete items as they run out. For example, an appropriate blackboard menu may be used to display the luncheon specials or evening dinner offerings on a large chalkboard set on an easel or on the wall in your entryway or waiting room. Descriptive details about each entree may be included. Later, at the table, a smaller version on a chalkboard or other display card or paper menu can be used, giving just names of entrees, desserts, and prices. This allows extra time for people to decide in advance what they will order. If an entree or other item runs out part way through the mealtime, it can be easily lined out or erased from the several menus.

A blackboard menu affixed to the wall will usually not offer a good view from every table in the dining room, and is therefore not recommended. Even one with good placement and legibility will not help the patron who has forgotten his glasses.

A blackboard menu offers several advantages, if the fare is consistently good. It adds spontaneity to the dining experience and allows people to develop confidence in the chef, rather than in the menu.

NAMING YOUR RESTAURANT

What restaurant name will you choose to make famous by your efforts? If there are more than two people involved in choosing the name, it may take months to arrive at a consensus. If your place is known for its excellent food and service, it will not matter what you have called it. And no matter how distinguished the name you choose, it will be forgotten if there is no distinctive quality in the food and its presentation.

The name of your restaurant should be consistent with the atmosphere you wish to establish in the dining room. A name that incorporates your family name or first name may give you recognition and ego gratification, but may also make the business harder to sell someday. You won't last forever, you know, and you may need to sell out. Long names will be shortened by your customers in word-of-mouth recommendations, and also by local businesspeople who may refer their customers to you. Therefore, be sure that none of the likely short-form names can be twisted into something uncomplimentary, ridiculous, or easily confused with any other business in the vicinity. In small towns, restaurant names of one, two, or three words are preferable, with not too many polysyllabic ones. But in the city you can get away with almost anything that will differentiate you from the crowd.

Give much consideration to the graphic representation of your name for signs and printed material. Again, it is worth hiring a graphic artist to design a tasteful logo for your business cards and advertising.

4.   Kitchen Design

THERE ARE professional restaurant designers who charge a lot of money to design a kitchen. But you should be able to do a good job on your own, with some advice. No kitchen will be perfect, but any kitchen that is reasonably well planned will serve, once the staff gets used to its limitations and idiosyncracies.

The final layout of your kitchen will be determined by the configuration of your building and by the type of food you wish to serve. If you are planning to work in a limited space that offers little flexibility, you may benefit from consulting an architect who has had experience in designing or remodeling other restaurants. (It helps if he's worked in a restaurant, too!)

Your first goal is to design a kitchen in which the cooking, meal assembly, and dishwashing areas are each functionally self-sufficient. Most kitchens require one area in which hot foods are prepared and assembled and one or more areas in which cold foods and beverages are handled. The layout of work space and equipment within each functional area should allow the chef, kitchen helpers, and dishwasher to work without getting in each other's way, but still to coordinate their efforts efficiently. This means that the most repetitive movements of the workers should traverse the shortest distances between key equipment and people. Movement of the staff into and around the kitchen must follow safe traffic patterns. The layout should help—or at least not hinder—the kitchen and dining room workers in carrying out their basic tasks.

Although functional efficiency and smooth interaction of the staff are the predominant goals to be met, the kitchen design must not sacrifice ease of cleaning and maintenance, adequate ventilation and lighting, or convenience for delivery, unloading, and storage of foodstuffs and linens, to any of the other goals.

DESIGN GOALS

A. Functional self-sufficiency for each area

B. Safety in the kitchen traffic pattern

C. Optimal interaction between key staff roles
   1. Chef to server
   2. Chef to dishwasher
   3. Chef to assistants
   4. Server to dishwasher
   5. Server to busperson

D. Efficient food preparation with shortest path for most common routines

E. Ease of cleaning and maintenance

F. Convenient unloading and delivery reception area

G. Proper ventilation and lighting

TABLE 1. *Design Goals for a Commercial Kitchen*

THE KITCHEN FLOOR PLAN

Insofar as possible, the food prepared in each section of the kitchen should be produced from the resources available right in that area. Also, it is necessary for some areas of the kitchen to serve more than one function, particularly in the small restaurant. Table 2, on the following page, lists the major and minor functions to be accounted for in your kitchen and adjacent storage areas.

FUNCTIONAL AREAS

Pre-meal preparation	Meal assembly in response to orders
Side-dish assembly	
Dessert preparation & service	Specialized food preparation (sandwiches, wok cooking, pizza, barbecue, deep fat frying)
Ice making & storage	
Walk-in cold & frozen storage	
Dishwashing & pot washing	Dry storage
Maintenance supply & equipment storage	Clean & dirty linen storage
	Office space with couch & safe
Delivery reception & unloading	
Baking facility	Employee personal item area

TABLE 2. *Functional Areas of a Commercial Kitchen*

Equipment placement. Once you have decided on the type of kitchen equipment you will require and you are familiar with the measurements of the equipment available, the actual placement of the various pieces deserves a great deal of thought. If you are having a building designed for you, or are doing it yourself, it pays to visualize your kitchen space in several alternative layouts.

One way to do this without having an actual building is to make a number of cutouts (or templates) in the shapes of the different items of equipment you will have. These may then be arranged on a large sheet of cross-hatched paper on which you have outlined, on the same scale as your cutouts, the walls and doors of your kitchen. This is especially useful in the case where you have an existing building which you wish not to remodel. The disadvantage of this method for final layout is that the wall space above the equipment is not easy to visualize. You will have to plan your wall space using a front view cutout.

Even after you have arrived at a plan that you think will work well, you may find out that some equipment must be switched around once it is all in place in the kitchen. To facilitate this game, be sure to take very accurate measurements of any equipment you look at in a dealer's showroom or in a catalogue. Remember, all kitchen equipment must allow for cleaning underneath; usually at least six inches in required by the health code.

Several kitchen equipment and design considerations deserve special comment and caution in your efforts. The exhaust hood, for example, is one of the most expensive items in a kitchen, though it has no actual cooking function. This is the hood over the cooking area, with grease filters, exhaust fan, and, in many localities, automatic fire extinguishing equipment. If you are on a limited budget, do not attempt to install a stainless-steel hood; a simple galvanized metal one will do fine. But the size of the hood, its clearance above the floor level, and the design of the exhaust system and grease filters are all very important. The hood must extend on three sides beyond the end of the array of equipment under it, and it must have a firewall behind it.

Are you planning to serve deep-fried food? Deep fat fryers, especially gas-fired ones, are the most dangerous, the dirtiest, and the least necessary items in a fine restaurant kitchen. If you plan on having them, I urge you to reconsider your menu. I won't even go into the poor nutritional value of deep-fried foods. The special problems of grease accumulation on *everything*, the breakdown and rancidity of the fat, and the fire and burn hazards to kitchen employees, make the whole subject distasteful to discuss. If you decide that you must have this item, visit the local restaurant that makes the best fish and chips and the like, and discuss with the staff the operation and maintenance of deep fat fryers and fat filtration.

If you use a reach-in refrigerator with a glass door and a light inside, it makes a wonderful night light for the kitchen.

Are you planning to use an open-flame barbecue or grill, or a wall-mounted grill known as a "salamander"? Some locales now require such cooking equipment to have special air-pollution control devices installed in the exhaust system. You will need to check the requirements with the building department.

Your kitchen design usually begins from a floor plan. A good place to start is with the plan for the *floor surface* itself. Ceramic tile is the low-maintenance standby for commercial kitchen floors. Today you can pass inspection with an asphalt-vinyl tile in most places, but this tends to require more maintenance. If you use a cement slab floor, your chef and kitchen assistants will probably get varicose veins unless you top the area where they work with portable grids made from slats of hardwood or rubberized material. There are all sorts of new products, with high prices to match, that can reduce wear and tear on your feet and legs. (See Chapter 9, Maintenance, for more information on this subject.)

If you do not have a cement floor and are fortunate enough to have a basement under your kitchen, you can install a single *floor sink* below the floor level. Such a sink is required by health codes in most states to provide for a two-inch air gap under each condensation line and under the drain from the dishwasher. This air gap prevents contaminated water from entering a refrigerator or dishwasher in the unlikely event that the sewer line backs up. You will save much money if you can install one floor sink beneath the entire kitchen rather than separate ones under each piece of equipment. Of course, some jurisdictions will permit you to use an electric warmer device to evaporate the refrigeration condensate. This works quite well, especially for self-defrosting freezers.

In many places, the health inspector is authorized to carry a sidearm. More than one chef has cooked up a felonious assault in his kitchen, especially when the inspector showed up with an order to close it.

The grease interceptor. The location of your grease trap is very important for cleaning access. If your restaurant is in a place where it gets very cold in the winter, you should have the trap in a spot where it can be indoors or inside shelter of some sort. The main advantage of outdoor access is that the odor dissipates quickly and so the cleaning can be done at any time. The main advantage of indoor access, aside from wintertime convenience, is that the trap can more easily be placed in the wastepipe system at a point where it will do the most good, without being on the main drain to the street sewer. If it is on the main drain line, it will have to be larger, and all the waste water will go through it—not good. The grease interceptor should be on a line that drains the pot sinks and other similar waste water from the kitchen. With such placement of the trap, you can then instruct the kitchen staff to clean the greasiest equipment in that sink, whenever possible.

Local regulations may prescribe different or more strict requirements. It is possible that you will be forced to install a larger capacity trap than you really need, and the cast-iron monsters come at an incredibly high cost. Even a trap with a small capacity (expressed in pounds of grease or in a flow in gallons per minute) will suffice, if you are diligent in emptying it. The bigger the trap, the worse is the job of cleaning it. And even a large trap will not do the job if you do not clean it often enough. You may be able to convince the sewer inspector that you will do the job right and that he should allow you to install a smaller, less expensive grease trap. (The best method for cleaning a small grease trap is discussed in Chapter 9.)

ANALYZING STAFF INTERACTION

Once you have made a tentative layout of all your necessary equipment, you should examine carefully the limitations that are placed on the chef and on others who will work in the restaurant. Begin by considering the most important element—the interaction between the chef and servers.

Chef to server. The order tickets prepared by the server are placed on a device that allows the chef to scan all the current orders to see what is coming up next. This "buffer" mechanism allows the chef to perfect his timing, and results in all the dinners for a single table being served at the same time, even if one of the steaks was ordered well done. Sometimes this device is a horizontal wheel with little spring-loaded clips to hold the tickets. Or it can be just a long row of such clips on a piece of metal, mounted where the server can readily hang up the ticket and the chef can easily see what is written. In some places, the server simply puts the order ticket where the chef or an assistant can get it, and it is then placed where the chef can glance at it as often as necessary. The key here is how easy it is for the chef to read the order.

A second factor is the server's ability to quickly check the order ticket at the time the plates are picked up. The server must verify that the order is correctly filled, and must also refresh his or her memory of which plate goes to which person at the table. If plates are being put onto a tray or carried on the arm, the order of removal is important, especially if the dining room is crowded and access to the far side of the table is difficult.

A crucial factor in this interaction is the chef's ability to be heard when he calls the server's name to pick up an order. There are also innumerable signal devices that the chef can use, both auditory and visual ones. Ideally, the server should be made aware that the order is ready without the chef having to shout. The layout of the restaurant should allow the server to proceed to the pickup point, take the order ticket, pick up the meal plates, and deliver them, all in less than a minute. In sixty seconds, a hot meal loses little flavor or heat. In 180 seconds it can lose its "piping hot" quality, and the diner partially loses its initial delicious aroma as well. The main advantage of a small dining establishment is that it can fulfill this implied promise to its customers: hot food will be served hot and cold food will be served cold. Your servers must understand this principle. If you wish to infuriate a chef, design your kitchen so that orders cannot be picked up within forty-five seconds after the call.

Food assembly by servers. Look carefully at the layout of the work area where food is assembled by the server rather than by the chef. This includes ladling soup, grabbing salad and topping it with dressing, preparing drinks, and setting out side dishes such as bread. If you bake your own rolls or brown pre-baked ones, they must be easily accessible to this work area. Many desserts must be assembled by scooping frozen ingredients, adding whipped topping, or serving a single portion from a larger pan, and these can all be done here.

This work area can serve other functions when it is not in use during a mealtime. Specialized serving utensils can be brought to the area as needed, if they cannot be stored right there. The specific limitations of your kitchen will determine how much of this type of preparation and assembly can be done by a server instead of a chef's assistant.

The "pass through." One style of restaurant design makes use of an opening in the wall through which the chef passes food to the servers for delivery to the tables or counter. This design usually allows the servers' preparation and storage area to be right in the dining room, often in conjunction with a counter service operation.

The pass-through design often results in some of the more frustrating moments in the life of the hungry traveler: he can see what looks like his meal sitting in the pass through under the infrared heat lamps getting dry, while his waitress is off somewhere relieving a nicotine fit. When the plate is finally picked up and delivered to someone else, he views his false anticipation with mixed feelings. His relief at not being served an "old" meal is tempered by the sure knowledge that if she was gone for that long once, she will soon decide to disappear again or to take an order from the party of twelve that was just seated. And she will do so just ten seconds before the cook places his plate under the heat lamp.

The pass through does permit the chef a measure of control in keeping the plates where they are until they are properly garnished and ready for pickup. But it forces the chef to handle each plate one extra time just to place it on the pass-through shelf. It is also likely that the chef will pull the ticket—remove the order from the board—and place it next to the plates.

Although the pass through is often right up front, one can be designed for a small restaurant without having it visible from the dining room. A partition to block that view can also serve to hide the server station, where water, silverware, napkins, and perhaps coffee and tea service originate.

Swinging doors. The pass-through type of chef–server interface eliminates constant use of one of the more dangerous features of many restaurant designs—the swinging door. Most commercial kitchen health codes require that the kitchen be separated from the area where the general public traffic is. The swinging door is the answer to that requirement, because it effectively blocks the escape of kitchen noise, smell, and visibility to and from the dining room. But it also requires the server to juggle the plates, or the serving tray or cart, in negotiating that tricky obstacle. The best to be said about such doors is that it is better to have two doors separated by a post so that one can be strictly for going in and the other strictly for going out. This traffic pattern is designed to avoid the inevitable collision that will occur if a single door is the only access. Swinging doors are now required to have a window at eye level containing safety (wire-mesh) glass for occupational safety reasons. But often the server or busperson with hands full will use a shoulder or backside to push open the door, and the window will not be looked at.

THE CHEF'S DOMAIN

I don't care who the owner is, the chef on duty is the boss in the kitchen.

The chef's domain is a tight concentration of cooking equipment, work space, refrigerated storage, heated storage (steam or dry table), and dish storage. Today's array of cooking equipment is likely to be centered on a large griddle and barbecue. At least one large microwave oven is necessary. Two are better. (Other microwave heating of desserts and bread may call for other oven units accessible to the servers.)

If you begin with a basic commercial oven, range, and griddle combination, you will find that a typical configuration houses two side-by-side ovens below and a combination of a griddle (available in widths that are multiples of twelve inches) and burners (in tandem units of two, front and back). For example, if you have space for a six-foot-wide range, you may have the top portion divided into six burners and a thirty-six-inch griddle, to the right or left. Or you could have a forty-eight-inch griddle coupled with four burners. When making the exact measurements for installation, be sure to allow sufficient access on the griddle side of the range to permit removal of the griddle grease waste trough and proper cleaning of the excess drippings.

It is not absolutely necessary to use a combination range. If you wish to set up the roasting ovens separately, the other cooking surfaces can be placed on storage stands or metal tables.

Plate storage. The "oven below" configuration makes it possible to keep dinner plates warm during the serving hours. But it increases the labor of the chef or assistant to have to open the oven door and pull out the plates while bending down. Overhead storage of the plates, on the other hand, may interfere with the exhaust of the grease-laden cooking fumes; and the shelf under the hood will accumulate enormous amounts of grease, creating an extra cleaning problem.

The best place for storage of plates used by the chef is opposite the cooking surfaces in a device that can warm the plates if necessary and also present them at waist-high level. These "plate elevators" have spring-loaded plate holders in a well such that as each plate is removed from the top of the pile the rest of the pile is raised up to allow the next plate to be grabbed easily. Plate elevators save a lot of wear on the chef.

It is important for the plate storage area to be handy to the dishwasher, so that replenishment is accomplished with minimal interference with the chef. Pot and pan storage is another consideration, but it is less critical than plate storage, for obvious reasons.

Chef's sink and supplies. There should be at least a small sink close to the chef, if possible, along with a work surface for a cutting board and knife rack. Other cooking and serving utensils of many varieties should hang within easy reach and should be easy to pick out from the entire array. If possible, the walk-in refrigerator and freezer should not be too far from the chef's position as well. The size of the chef's working refrigerator—the reach-in one—will determine how often it must be replenished during the mealtime. It should be large enough to allow the meat and fish cuts that are most used to be stored in the trays on which they were placed during initial portion preparation.

The time and energy of the chef will be conserved to the extent that it is possible to store at about waist- to eye-level height the items that he or she must use for each dinner plate. The more times each day that the chef must reach overhead or bend to below the knees, the fewer will be his or her active years as a chef.

Steam table. Most hot-food storage tables can be operated with or without water. A dry table keeps trays hot without too much dehydration unless you are serving for long hours without using up the food. (If that is the case, you are in big trouble.) The specific configuration of the steam table or dry table can be arranged to fit your menu needs. Typically, it holds deep bains-marie, or tublike containers, for soup and rice. It can also be set up to hold hot pots of sauce or gravy. Shallow trays for such items as lasagna, eggplant Parmegiana, or baked chicken can be taken directly from the oven and placed under a stainless-steel cover right in the steam table. The size of this type of unit will depend on the amount of space you have for it. The minimum width that is practical for general use is four feet, but it is nice to have an extra twelve to twenty-four inches in your steam table just in case you need it.

Baking ovens. All good restaurants do some baking—either of desserts, or of other products made with flour. A pastry table with a laminated wood surface (butcher-block style) is the sign of such a work area. Some bakers swear by the so-called convection oven for making pies and, especially, pastries. This is an oven in which the circulation of heated air is directed more evenly throughout by electric fans, even if the heat source is gas-fired. Some people believe that this type of oven cuts baking time so much that it constitutes a significant saving in energy. But these considerations may apply more to a bakery than to your small restaurant. In any case, many are the delicious pies that have emerged from the conventional roasting oven, which can also be used for other purposes.

SPECIALIZED EQUIPMENT

If your menu and volume of business require special kitchen devices, you will want to position them as close as possible to their functional work area. Such items might include a twelve- to twenty-quart mixer, electric slicer, meat grinder, can opener (for large cans), blender, refrigerated milk dispenser, bread and bun warmers, warming oven for prime rib or roast meat storage (handy for a small place where the prime rib is an important specialty requiring several roasts each night), special "broasters," steamers for shellfish, pizza ovens, and the like.

If your menu includes sandwiches you may find it convenient to have a sandwich-maker unit, which consists of a refrigerator below and a cold tray above in which small stainless-steel inserts hold the various ingredients. The unit also has a narrow wooden or plastic cutting surface running along the entire front edge. The contents of the stainless-steel inserts are kept cool during the meal preparation period by the refrigeration coils below. When not in use, the sandwich makings can be placed inside the reach-in underneath. The assembly of trays is protected by a metal shelf and hinged cover, which drops down to preserve the lower temperature between orders. The unit is designed to be a complete preparation center and is available in lengths from thirty-six inches to more than six feet. It may suit your purposes very well, in combination with a plate storage shelf and bread storage. If you have an extensive sandwich trade, you probably need one at least four feet wide.

The commercial toaster is a vital part of the lunch business and is an absolute necessity for any breakfast menu. The pop-up type that handles four slices at a time is the most reliable, but is expensive to purchase or to renovate. The last time I priced the timer for one side of a Toastmaster commercial toaster (there are two timers in each four-slice machine) it was about $25. There should be space for your toaster(s) immediately adjacent to the sandwich assembly unit.

FOOD STORAGE

Storage for staple food items is always in short supply. It is most logical to have a delivery entrance, with easy access from the street or alley, near the main storage room or area. If for some reason this storage area is in a basement or loft, the access should include if at all possible some sort of ramp or conveyance on which the heavy cartons can be moved directly into the storage space without having to be carried up or down a staircase. For more economical purchasing, it is best to have storage barrels that will hold fifty- or hundred-pound sacks of staples such as rice, pastry flour, and sugar. In the kitchen itself there should be shelf space for at least one or two spare cans and boxes of items used constantly, even if the principal storage area is elsewhere.

The health code permits some types of storage areas to be used only if no opened items are kept there. Otherwise, the storage area must conform to the same strict floor and wall surface requirements that apply to the food preparation areas. Rodent and vermin control is unquestionably the worst problem in the use of a remote storage facility. If you are contemplating remodeling an old building, remember that the mice already know it better than you do. Make a very thorough inspection of the foundation and crawl spaces under the floors, if any, and of all places where pipes or conduits enter the building. Even the smallest openings must be sealed with quarter-inch wire mesh.

ICE

There is an endless need for ice in any restaurant. Icemakers for cubes, cubelets, flakes, or chips are available in all sizes, from the one that dispenses a few tablespoons into a soft-drink glass up to the bin with a 2,000-pound capacity. The prices seem to begin at around $1,200 for anything worth having. The cubelet is most practical, unless you have a frequent need to pack all sorts of dishes in a cold buffet table for a large banquet type of setting; flaked ice is best for that. The location of your ice machine should allow for runoff of the overflow of water used to flush the machine, as well as the normal cycling overflow. From that location, bins of ice can be dispersed to other parts of the restaurant where they are needed. Remember that if you choose to put your machine outside for some reason, it will have to be protected from vandalism during nonbusiness hours.

DISH AND POT WASHING

The placement of your dishwashing and potwashing equipment deserves careful thought. Besides bearing in mind both the plumbing and the ventilation of the area, you should try to place it where dirty dishes can be returned from the dining room without going through the main part of the kitchen. If you possibly can, route the dirty dish return path so that it does not coincide with that taken by the servers carrying full plates to the dining room.

If you will use an automatic dishwashing machine, the space for it must include room to hold several waiting trays of dirty dishes and pots and pans without cluttering up the access to the area. It must also allow sufficient space for the dishwasher racks that hold the dirty dishes, glasses, and silverware to be set up for filling; and there must still be adequate space for the plates to be scraped and pre-rinsed. The secret of good dishwashing is to place the dishes in the racks with as few food particles on them as possible, and to pre-soak any utensil that has dried food residue on it. If the input side of the setup permits proper sorting, soaking, scraping, and stacking of dirty dishes, silverware, and cups and glasses, then the loading of the dishracks can be done so as to permit easy unloading on the output side of the machine. On a busy night when you discover that you are running out of dinner forks and wine glasses, you will appreciate having a well-organized dishroom.

Automatic dishwashers for restaurants have two cycles. The wash cycle causes soapy water at 160° F to be forcefully sprayed all over the contents of the machine for about two and a half minutes. After a short pause, clean water at 170° to 180°, containing a rinsing and drying agent, is sprayed over the dishes. The dishrack should then be removed from the machine and let stand so the dishes may air-dry and cool. The space on the output side must therefore be adequate to allow several racks to stand. Some dishwashing machine setups include angled shelves over the drainboard specifically for the purpose of holding drying and cooling racks. This arrangement lets you sort the contents of outcoming trays and reassemble them in the cooling racks. For example, if you hold partially filled racks of glasses until a full tray can be carried out to the glass storage area, it allows the glasses to be properly cooled before use; at the same time it reduces congestion on the input side, because the glasses can be washed with other items in a rack and you don't have to wait for a full rack of dirty glasses to accumulate.

But luxuries such as special shelves are not necessary for a good dishwashing operation. If there is enough drainboard counter space on both sides of the machine, any clever dishwasher will be able to develop a satisfactory routine. Finally, be certain that your plumbing plan for the dishwashing area includes a water hose connection, so that you can use a short hose to rinse out the bottom of the machine.

Your early planning activities should include detailed inspections of the dishwashing setups at several busy restaurants. Machines may also be leased if you cannot afford the capital outlay to buy one at first. And be certain, if you are building or remodeling to create your restaurant, that the electrician has experience in hooking up electrical service for automatic dishwashers. It is not a simple matter and has important safety considerations, especially if you have a food grinder with an electrically switched water valve.

If you choose to wash dishes manually, you may still benefit from the use of a few plastic dishwasher racks for holding your dishes while they dry and for dipping clean dishes in the disinfectant solution contained in the third tub of the required three-tub sink. You may have to pay a higher wage to get someone to do the work properly. And rubber gloves are a must to protect the hands of your dishwasher. In fact, you may wish to discuss the effects of your soap solution and disinfectant rinse with a local dermatologist and your insurance man before you decide not to spend the money for a machine. You would be surprised at how small some of those automatic dishwashers are. Of course, there are energy-saving aspects to the old manual method.

Pot washing. Most health codes recognize that the automatic dishwashing machine will not serve for the larger pots used in restaurant cooking. Investigate early the local requirements for having a pot sink. In some jurisdictions, a three-tub sink is required for disinfecting your pots. Even in the absence of such a rule, however, you may be required to have a sink that is large enough in which to immerse your largest pots; and most codes do require a double sink. It is possible to get a big pot clean in a single sink. The key is good scrubbing materials, a thorough person wielding them, and plenty of hot water, preferably dispensed through a sprayer device.

LINEN STORAGE

The linen storage area in a restaurant must be convenient to both the kitchen and the dining room. The kitchen linen area must have clean towels, cloths, aprons, griddle wipes, and also space for the bin or bags in which dirty kitchen and dining room linens can be placed for pickup by your linen service. The linen service will expect you to keep table linen separate from the dirtier kitchen linen. You will need space in the dining room to store unfolded as well as folded napkins and tablecloths. When the tables are cleared you may save steps for the busperson by having a dirty table linen bin somewhere close to the dining room.

OFFICE AND EMPLOYEE AREA

Leave room for an office. Please. You must have a place on the premises to file your invoices, keep your checkbook and extra cash, and talk privately with employees and salesmen. If possible, you should have room in the office for a cot or six-foot couch. The list of items for the office or some place in the kitchen is endless, but it includes at least the following: adding machine, cookbooks, first-aid supplies, aspirins, telephone and list of frequently called numbers, employee time sheets, schedule sheets, masking tape, and the other innumerable items of office supply. Everything cannot be stored under a counter somewhere.

Whether or not the local health code requires it, you must also establish a spot where your employees can put personal garments so that they are not in contact with food preparation areas. This employee area must also provide a safe storage place for personal valuables such as women's purses. This means that a row of hooks near the delivery entrance, where any delivery person can take something from a purse without being observed, is unsatisfactory for handbags, though it may serve all right for coats. A large shelf inside the office near the time sheet is the best place for purse storage. You will also expect your servers to be responsible for having clean aprons or uniforms, if you use them. A small locker or clothes hanger bar where employees can keep their aprons or uniform parts separate from someone else's is also helpful.

WORKING WITH LESS THAN PERFECTION

Your kitchen will hardly be perfect. You will find it difficult to implement all the suggested relationships among functional areas and people, even in a brand new building. But even in the most badly arranged kitchen it is possible to make excellent food. It just comes at a cost you may not be willing to pay for more than a year or two, in terms of added stress, fatigue, accidents, and frustration. If it is possible to make some changes to improve the work flow in an existing kitchen by remodeling before you open, it will be worth doing. If the kitchen design allows smooth operation, it affects every aspect of the restaurant. What could be more basic than that?

5.   What the Public Sees

THIS BOOK emphasizes the fine, small dinner house, implying comfort with style, moderate to high price structure, and complete dinners, selected perhaps from a relatively limited menu each night. The reasons for this focus are, in part, connected with the lasting demand everywhere for such good restaurants, and the potential for earning enough from even a small place to make the enterprise economically and psychologically feasible. Also, this emphasis allows the author certain economies in describing basic principles and practices that apply just as well to other restaurant styles. This chapter focuses on topics in the context of a wider range of restaurant styles, because the dining room of a small establishment is the feature most likely to vary with the type of food and service.

FURNISHINGS FOR THE DINING ROOM

Tables. The diner in a typical restaurant sits at a table designed to serve four people comfortably; some of the other tables in the place are sized for two and for six or more persons. Various methods can be used to extend the standard size table to seat more people, but few serve as well as using a table that is already the right size for the party.

The table surface finish must allow the tabletop to be kept free from accumulated food and liquid residues; and the top must be affixed so that the table does not tip over. The top may be a simple unfinished piece of plywood, to be covered at all times by a thin padding and a tablecloth. Or it may be an elegant and imaginatively handcrafted surface, fitting the theme of your restaurant. Some overworked examples of the latter are hatch-cover tabletops for oyster bars or fish houses, and transparent resin-coated tops in which theme flora and fauna or other artifacts have been captured. But I have also seen artistically laminated or bolted-together materials used to create durable and interesting tabletops, including several with wrought-iron frames.

To provide ease in seating and in moving around the table, the top should be supported by a pedestal in the center, resting on a heavy base or with low, widespread supporting feet. If a booth arrangement is used, the table may even be inserted in a flange bolted to the floor, although this limits both its movability for cleaning and its adjustment for large people. Tables with legs attached at or near the corners are more stable than the pedestal type, but the legs interfere with chairs, especially if two or more tables are pushed together to accommodate a large group.

Older tables that look like or are antiques allow you to use an assortment of designs in the same room, and may contribute added interest to your dining area. But before you buy antiques or any other used tables, inspect them carefully for damage that might snag clothing or affect the table's sturdiness or strength. The tabletop finish can always be renewed—even with plastic finish material. Good used tables may be purchased for as little as $60 or $70; but antiques could cost as much as $500 each. You may do best by combining used pedestal bases with new tops, either commercially available or handcrafted.

Seating. Chairs must be comfortable for at least the duration of a typical meal. And the chair size must permit the average customer to fit under your tables. The normal table measures twenty-six to twenty-eight inches from the floor to the underside of the tabletop. The typical chair seat is sixteen to eighteen inches above the floor. An eight-inch thigh space is enough.

The chairs you select should have the following features:

- A pleasing style consistent with your table and room decor.
- Adequate comfort for their intended duration of use.
- The strength to stand up under hard use even by an enormous patron.
- Durability for cleaning and resistance to stains and development of rough edges.
- Overall size that does not restrict your use of limited space in the dining room—for server and patron movement, aisles, and placement of enough tables to justify the overhead costs for the space.

The last condition mentioned is most easily met by the less formal style of chair, done in a combination of metal and modern synthetic coverings. Unfortunately, this coffee-shop type of chair does not always fit the style of an interesting small restaurant. Good wooden chairs, perhaps with padded seats of some sort, come in a variety of styles and finishes.

I have heard too many complaints about the chairs in otherwise good, new small restaurants to recommend that you try to skimp on the chair budget. It may pay to purchase new chairs to ensure your meeting all of the above criteria. Even good used chairs can cost more than eighty dollars apiece at an auction if they have a pleasing design and are in good to excellent condition. Consider buying more chairs than you need at first, since you may get a better price per chair. If you have a place to store the extras, you may appreciate having them on hand later for a room you add on or to replace unserviceable chairs.

If you are on a tight budget, however, you may find a good buy in chairs that would serve well if completely refurbished. Or you may economize in a less formal style by purchasing sets of chairs that do not all match but provide a set for each table. This works very well with antiques.

If yours is a more informal restaurant, you might take a simple chair design and build your own seating that will serve to get you started. If you plan to replace them later on, be sure to get candid comments from your customers on how comfortable they find the seats. Then act accordingly.

Booth seating offers the patron more privacy and greater seat cushioning at the expense of formality in service and your flexibility in changing the dining room layout. For less formal restaurants, booths do offer an excellent alternative to finding enough good used chairs or buying expensive new ones. Some semicircular booths hold six to eight persons comfortably. If booths fit your plans, you may wish to have them made to order for size and color. Or sometimes restaurant auctions or dealers will have excellent buys in used booths, with or without matching tables. You will need to match the dimensions of your dining room aisle and wall space with those of the booths for sale. In this regard, remember that you can fill a few feet of space between booths with conveniently placed storage for trays and tableware, or with a server station.

For some styles of restaurant, even the lowly bench may serve the purpose, especially for outdoor use, informal family-style service at long tables, or the like.

Counter service. Even the best gourmet menu does not preclude serving the meal at a counter. The informality of a counter allows a single diner to eat his meal in the company of others, and, if the counter itself does not take up space better used for tables or other essential furniture, it can increase the number of meals served and your customer turnover. If single patrons are willing to sit at a counter, it makes for more efficient use of your tables. A counter may even suggest special uses such as serving hors d'oeuvres, shellfish, juice, or salads. It may be limited to the service of soup and sandwiches, or beverages and desserts, where tables are reserved for the longer, more complete meals during the peak hours. Or it may simply offer the more traditional alcoholic beverage service, with food service at the bar as an option for the customer.

The bar or counter itself may be of unique design or historical interest, or it may offer the patron a perch from which to observe and converse with the chef during the preparation of special food, as at an oyster bar or with the traditional Japanese sushi. If you use the modern swivel stools with small backrests you need not give up comfort even at a counter.

If you are planning to open at the site of a former restaurant that has a counter, think carefully about what use you might make of it before you decide to tear it out. Use your imagination. Moving it to a different position, perhaps even into the waiting area, and installing some interesting feature for your patrons to look at over a glass of wine might just make your place the most unusual one in town. Consider stained glass if you put the counter near a window with good light. Or a large fish tank might serve in a similar fashion; in some cities such tanks are available on a rental basis, including regular servicing as well as the fishy tenants.

Outdoor service. The opportunity to take a meal or to sip a refreshing drink in a relaxed outdoor setting is all too infrequently available in this country. If your restaurant overlooks the sea, a lake, a garden, or a valley, the unobstructed view or feeling of openness can make your place better than the competitors', even where the outdoor season is short.

If you decide to serve outdoors, you must consider the effects of direct sunlight, which can be devastating to most table and chair finishes. The effects of moisture and temperature changes are even more obvious. Laminated wood will come apart and warp unless the wood was very well dried and treated before lamination. Most resin or plastic finishes, or glued-on material such as Formica intended for indoor use, will cloud, crack, peel, disintegrate, or all of the above. Eventually all colors will turn into weathered gray, especially on wooden furniture and the canvas seats and backs of folding director's chairs. Oxidation of metal will render some surfaces unable to meet the minimum sanitary standards set for food service.

But these and other problems of outdoor service, such as the regulations of alcoholic beverage control, health departments, and zoning inspectors, can usually be solved by careful planning and the use of materials that are designed to withstand the effects of weather. Winter storage facilities are a great help. Awnings, sunshades, and wind screens offer protection to both furniture and patrons. And regular painting, resurfacing, and refinishing of tables, seats, and serving surfaces will prolong the life of your outdoor equipment.

In Europe, even where there is a short summer season, outdoor eating areas are a popular adjunct to restaurants. The United States has lagged in this development for some reason. We would rather eat in a windowless room filled with smoke. No wonder we are hyperactive, and suffer from stress-induced diseases.

Accommodating children and infants. High chairs are an invitation to those patrons who otherwise might not frequent your establish-

mean that you should stick to bare walls. Rather, make use of
rrors to lighten some darker corners; cover the wall surface closest
the tabletops and seats with a suitable finish for constant
nsing; and limit your theme artifacts or artwork to a tasteful
tion of a few items, instead of crowding your entire collection
he room at one time. If you are fortunate enough to own a large
nteresting collection of objects of historical or aesthetic interest,
teady customers as well as your staff will appreciate them more
periodically change the display rather than plastering the
nd ceiling with it.

Whatever decorations or display you employ must be kept
nd dust-free. A dusty or grimy looking antique does not
te the appetite, nor does a musty drapery or curtain. Even a
icture or sign loses its impact if it turns out to be covered
t or fly specks when one gets close. (I don't know which is
have in a restaurant dining room, live flies or dead ones on
wsill. Live ones make me wonder about the kitchen, but
make me wonder what killed them and how long since the
last cleaned.)

ossible, have one or more tables in your room that are
shielded from other tables, where parties with small
n be seated. This will allow you to move anyone who is
a fussy child to another table. You could make good use
le screen under such circumstances, if you have a nice
reen can also be used when a larger party desires some
rom the rest of the room and you do not have a private
purpose. (But make sure that any free-standing screen

hould be legible from across the room, even at night.
oint in marking directions to the rest rooms if your
most patrons having to ask for directions anyway. The
ations will prescribe exit signs.

---

the temptation to use items like old beautiful
, bud vases, or antique saltcellars unless you are
to part with them. They may not be pilfered. But
obably will be chipped, cracked, or broken by a
ning but clumsy dishwasher.

ment. Your tolerance for the problems that go along with serving
infants and toddlers will determine whether you use and retain this
type of seat. If you do provide high chairs, be certain you have both a
safe place to store them when not in use, and sufficient space at
some of your tables to set up the chair where the child can neither
grab at a server carrying hot food nor be tripped over. Old wooden
high chairs are nice, but they cost a lot of money these days. The new
types may offer the convenience of fold-away storage as well as a
more easily cleanable surface finish.

Seating for the somewhat older child who is too big for a high
chair but too small for the regular seat presents a potential safety
problem. The traditional padded booster device, resembling a small
hassock with a little rounded back, is designed for use *only* in a
booth. It should not be used on a chair that does not have side arms
to prevent its tipping over and allowing the child to fall. If you do not
have a youth chair (a higher chair without a tray) that can be moved
right up to the table, try the old telephone book trick or something
similar, to raise the youngster enough to eat comfortably but not
precariously.

Other dining room needs. It is impractical to have to carry water
from the kitchen to the table. Even if you cannot provide the
plumbing to allow your servers to conveniently fill a pitcher right in
the dining room, it is essential that you have a place for filled water
pitchers and storage for clean water and wine glasses in the dining
area. The same holds true for cups and saucers for tea or coffee. It is
a great convenience to have an ice receptacle in the dining room, as
well as conveniently placed coffeepot and hot water burners.

The need for clean tableware and linen for setting the tables is
never ending. If you use tablecloths, they must be stored nearby, yet
not in a place where they may be splashed by liquids or food
particles. The same goes for other place setting items, such as paper
placemats and paper napkins. If you regularly use small dishes for
your place settings, such as butter plates, these should be stored for
easy access when setting up a table. Be sure to provide a place for
serving trays to go when not in use, as well as a spot to hold wet wipe
cloths out of sight of the patrons. You may also want a place for
special condiments that are not always on the table, such as
mustard, catsup, salsa, hot sauce, syrups, vinegar and oil, relish, or
what have you.

All these needs may require you to build special shelves and cupboards; or you might take the opportunity to add some interesting or antique piece of furniture that will give a touch of hominess to the room. A sea captain's chart desk might serve to hold some of the items mentioned as well as menus and wine lists. Or perhaps the large old sideboard that Grandma almost gave away because it was too big for her apartment will get a new lease on life.

Visit the local antique shops on your day off. A beautiful piece will often fit into almost any small restaurant's decor and can serve you well for storage and delight your customers too. Moreover, the shop owner may be smart enough to give you a "business discount" if your restaurant caters to the antique buying public.

Self-service equipment. The popular self-service salad bars— including those with places for soup tureens, hot bread or rolls, butter, and all the dressings and garnishes that go with salads—are becoming more and more commonplace. (They may have been side-tracked somewhat by the winter of 1977-1978, when the price of iceberg lettuce hit $30 or more for a case of twenty-four heads.) Your plans may include the use of such self-service equipment, or something similar for making your own ice-cream sundaes or cooking your own stir-fried meal or making your own veggie or fruit drink in a blender/juicer. Who knows what fads the future holds?

Your decision to use this equipment will be of great interest to the local health inspector. He or she will be concerned about what provision you make for what is commonly known as a "sneeze guard." It is also called a "breath barrier," and probably other names I haven't yet heard of. This transparent barrier must stand between the patrons' faces and any uncovered food, to block the transfer of germs from the breath to the common pot. It must be wide enough to work for various sizes of people while not obstructing the view of what you are trying to serve. Such barriers have been in use for years in cafeterias where individual portions of food, such as salads and desserts, are available for selection in an unwrapped condition. But they present a particularly awkward problem for serve-yourself bars, which have already been outlawed completely in many places as an insurmountable health hazard.

DINING ROOM DECOR

I have no intention of discussing all the possib design for restaurants; I am not an expert on this likely to be of much help with any specific styl however, to understand a few principles in adva sense and powers of observation have not evident.

• *Your dining room layout should affor room, if possible, from one or two vantage entrance.* This will enable the manager respond to needs not always evident to the s dividers, half-walls, and structural supp therefore, should create a feeling of c without actually cutting up the room int of appropriate potted plants rather pathways within the dining area is som natural method. Plants can also screen area or a less attractive serving statio

• *The lighting in your dining roo mood, and should be augmented whe ramp occurs.* The natural light from preferable to excessive reliance on switches for your incandescent lig daytime to an evening mood. The effects of light on mammals, the even for very informal dining glaring light from any source by deflect, or block it. In short, it lighting design of as many commit yourself to an electric in fixtures.

• *Heating and cooling tables to an extreme.* This i yet it is commonly ignore table. How will you feel seated an anonymous but table with an intolerable

• *Your wall spac reflector of light and co*

No smoking? The battle is on between those who insist that it is a human right to smoke anywhere (except where it constitutes a fire hazard) and those who consider other people's smoke a health hazard to everyone. You are right in the middle of one of the strategic battlefields. A careful reading of the local smoking regulation and method of enforcement is the place to start.

The rules of war in your locale may require you to reserve a significant portion of your dining room for those who are annoyed by smoking. Even if this is not required, it is a good solution if you have the room. Put up a sign, or ask each party as they arrive if they prefer a no-smoking section. Your best weapon may be a quiet, but very effective exhaust system for the dining room. When the smoke clears, however, you don't want any casualties—that is, you want both the smokers and the nonsmokers to realize that you have done your best to allow them to enjoy their meals.

You will have difficulty moving the unhappy occupants of a table to another one after they are seated. The smoker will say, "Let *them* move—I was here first." The customer who is allergic to smoke will say, "I am the one being made ill and if I have to move, I will simply leave and never return." Separate sections in a large enough dining room evades this confrontation, as in an airliner, but it doesn't help you if your room is small and poorly ventilated.

What can you do? Do not supply the "arms." Do not sell cigarettes or cigars in your restaurant; offer matches only on request, but cheerfully provide an ashtray to protect your table and carpet when a smoker asks for one or lights up without one. Display a sign that states what the local ordinance requires, such as no smoking in rest rooms. *Enforce strictly the universal health standard for food service personnel that prohibits use of tobacco in any form while working with or near food.*

In our restaurant waiting room we displayed a sign in a somewhat florid calligraphy that said, "Thank You for Not Smoking." Most people took it to mean that smoking was prohibited. Smokers often asked if that were the case, and were told, "You are permitted to smoke, but naturally in our small dining room we don't encourage it." To mollify them, I was able to take advantage of the calligraphic resemblance of the "M" to "N" and of the "K" to "R" and to tell them that on busy nights many waiting people read the sign as "Thank You for Not Snoring."

THE CASHIER STATION AND WAITING ROOM

The cashier station is where you will carry out all the tasks related to checking the customers' bills, making change, and preparing and verifying transactions with credit cards, travelers checks, and personal checks, if you accept them. Here you may wish to provide space, and electrical outlets, for special lighting, an electric cash register, an electric calculator, a credit-card imprinter, controls for your music system, a paging system, an intercom with the kitchen or other key points in the restaurant, a telephone jack, and a special safe or lockable built-in drawer for holding extra cash or deposits separately from the receipts in the cash drawer. When the cashier operation is combined with handling reservations, the space must be larger, and you will need to be able to see and communicate with the dining room. Most small restaurants combine these operations at or near the front entrance or exit.

If the cash drawer is in the area where patrons wait to be seated, a logical use of the host's time when there are no tables available is to have him handle the cashier job. But you may deliberately separate the cash drawer from the waiting room, for safety, for the convenience of the servers, or because of space limitations. I have found that it is best to limit the handling of the money to as few people as practical. Variations from this practice depend on the style of the restaurant and also on how busy it is. The less formal the meal, the more likely it is that the cash drawer will be manned by whomever has the time at the moment the customer is ready to pay.

The busier your restaurant, the more likely it is that you can afford a full-time cashier or host/cashier. The cashier can also double as bartender, busperson, table setter, take-out clerk, or regular server for a station, such as a counter, that is near the cash drawer. If your waiting room is the site for any tie-in retail sales such as take-home food, jewelry, or souvenirs, it is natural for the cashier to handle that operation.

If you do not use a cash register that produces some sort of printed record of your sales, you should consult your accountant or tax adviser about what methods to use to verify your sales volume, both for income tax and state sales tax purposes.

Certain tie-in sales in a restaurant may present special cases for segregating those records and receipts from your table service or consumption-on-premises sales. If your cash register does not have the means for entering a code while ringing up the sale, you may choose to employ entirely separate registers. Examples of such sales include cases where state sales or meals tax applies to the food served or consumed on the premises, but not to food, like bakery or delicatessen items, sold for use at home. Your financial adviser or accountant will know what methods for keeping records and receipts are most practical and acceptable to the tax people.

There is something to be said for the system used in Europe: the customer pays the server, who carries his own change and makes it, and the server is then responsible for paying the house for every item of food or drink served. It reduces "arithmetic errors" that are otherwise absorbed by the owner.

What about all those people in the waiting room? Some restaurant owners I know would love to have that problem. It is best solved before it occurs, by making sure the size of your waiting area is adequate. You should provide seats for a reasonable number of people—about five to eight seats for a forty-seat restaurant. The benches or chairs should be placed so that they do not interfere with patrons who are there to pay the cashier, or with servers delivering a check or payment to the cashier. The seats should not impede the normal traffic through the entry area.

Besides capacity, you want the area to make a pleasing first impression on new customers. It can be more than just an all-weather room for a short wait for a table. Set up your entry room so that a customer coming in on a busy night will naturally gravitate to the host or cashier and give his name and the number in his party, or ask the inevitable "How long is the wait for a table for two?"

One way to pay for the cost of a larger entry area is to plan for display cases for small but high-priced items you can sell to those who spend time in the room. (A lighted case is very desirable at night.) Almost any interesting handcrafted item or collectible, whether new or antique, is suitable. Maybe your own hobby fits the bill. Miniature soldiers, scale-model trains, dolls, clocks, hand-blown glassware, spoon collections, dollhouse furniture, old documents—the list is virtually endless, and it doesn't have to tie' in with your restaurant name, style of food, or service. It just has to be interesting, unique, or scarce, and not cheap or tacky.

WHAT ABOUT REST ROOMS?

Countless satisfied customers have commented on how nice and clean our rest rooms were, and how often they judge the attitude of a restaurant by that observation.

I find it insulting to the public that food service establishments in some states do not provide a place for their customers to wash their hands before eating (and are not required by law to do so). Rather than argue the point, I will merely state that you have as much obligation to satisfy your customers' hygienic needs as you do to meet their need for nourishment and physical comfort. To me, this means you must have a clean public toilet and sink. The health regulations already require no less for your employees.

Those jurisdictions that require rest rooms for both patrons and employees often also require a vestibule between the rest room door and the dining room or kitchen. In some locales, this requirement is being eliminated for the dining room access. (See below for some uses you can make of such vestibules.) Local regulations will influence the number and placement of your rest rooms, and, in many cases, what their minimum area must be. Some building codes stipulate how the air in the rest rooms shall be exhausted, how the fan motor and light switch shall be interconnected, and so on to the point where you may wish you could avoid installing a bathroom altogether.

How many? For a small restaurant, you do not need a large rest room, but you can always use more than one, even if the regulation says you can get away with only one for your seating capacity. So if you have the space, it may be better to remodel a large rest room into two or three smaller ones.

If your rest room capacity is one person at a time, I see no good reason for designating one room for men and the other for women. Passenger aircraft rest rooms serve very well without such restrictions. Try doing something more practical, such as installing a special grab rail for older people and small children, next to a pedestal toilet, which is higher than the conventional toilet. The pedestal toilet is easier for arthritics and handicapped people to use. And remember to allow room for wheelchairs when designing the door width. Dispensing with "men" and "women" signs improves the availability of rest rooms when the demand is unbalanced. Besides, I believe that it discourages graffiti. Maybe not.

Regardless of the number of rest rooms you provide, it helps to have the floors made of ceramic tile, with a good waterproof grout, so that you can keep them all as spotlessly clean as possible. It also helps to keep the walls painted so they can survive frequent wash-downs without pitting. And the bathroom decor ought to give a feeling of cleanliness, even if it also features decorator wallpaper on the ceiling. If you can afford it, install a ceramic tile wainscot behind the fixtures, especially if you have a men's urinal of any sort.

Urinals are useless. I do not recommend the use of urinals, primarily because some designs are useless for small boys, and because they are more of a nuisance to keep clean and sweet-smelling than are toilets. Aside from splashing problems, men are less likely to flush a urinal than a regular toilet. If you are concerned about the water consumption of toilets, there is a recently developed pressure-sensitive plastic valve that is easily installed in the toilet tank to replace the old ball float or flap device. This valve can be set for the amount of water you wish to use in the tank, and has found wide-spread use in motels. If you seek ways to conserve water, you will do better by replacing leaky faucet washers and instructing your dish-washing crew in conservation measures than by installing urinals.

Lighting and ventilation. Lighting in the rest room is just as important as in the kitchen, but it need not be glaringly bright. Let the light be adequate but not unflattering to the patron who checks to see how he or she looks in the mirror. Do provide mirrors, but keep them clean. It is nice to have a source of natural daylight in the rest room if you can; a skylight will serve where no outside wall is available.

A direct source of fresh outside air is also a desirable rest room feature, rather than having to rely on an exhaust fan. The air sucked into the rest room by such a fan usually comes from inside the building, where it has already become stale and laden with odors from cooking, smoking, and human bodies.

Rest room locks. Be prepared for little dramas to be acted out in your rest rooms. There is no lock or latch that will not confound someone. Most failures will revolve around an unlatched door leading to an embarrassment, but occasionally a small child will inadvertently lock himself in. A simple slide latch or hook is all that is really needed to indicate that the room is in use; stout locks are superfluous. Many jurisdictions do however require automatic door closers.

Making use of the rest room vestibule. Do not ignore your rest room vestibule when you plan your decor and obtain seats for the waiting room. The typical use for this spot, if it is large enough, is as a holding area for patrons waiting to use an occupied bathroom and as a place to install a public telephone. Some restaurant owners fill the extra space with a variety of machines for vending cigarettes, chewing gum, combs and handkerchiefs, souvenirs, and what have you. My personal favorite use of the wall space, even in a small vestibule, is to display information on the history of the restaurant building, the town, or the area, and to give directions to points of interest, or other data of an entertainment value.

ON MUSIC

If you have ever spent an evening in a small restaurant where your enjoyment of well-prepared, fresh food and stimulating conversation was completely negated by atrocious background music, then you appreciate the importance of music in a restaurant. With a happy choice of music to enhance their dining interlude, your patrons may well compliment the musical accompaniment even more than the chef's best efforts.

The effect of music on your chef, your staff, and yourself is of as much concern as its effect on your patrons in the dining room. After all, unlike the diners, you and your staff must endure the music all day and evening. Therefore, your system should allow you to select variety as well as to provide continuity.

The cost of a system that enables you to choose a daily variety of music will be a significant factor in your initial capital investment and operating budget. If you are fortunate enough to locate in an area with a broad range of offerings in FM radio programming, you may be able to take advantage of that resource. But the sooner you begin to think about and collect appropriate music on tape, even if it is just for emergency backup purposes, the better. This may mean that you ought to cultivate the friendship and assistance of a hi-fi buff with really good equipment.

The level of sound in a dining room is very important. Subtle differences in sound level can create or destroy your intended mood. Ever since the moguls of industry discovered that music affects human behavior, such as productivity or readiness to buy something, there have been systems designed to produce so-called background music. The music itself is supposed to be innocuous and the sound level is set so that you don't actually have to attend. In fact, if you want to listen, you must sometimes strain to hear. This kind of music serves the same function as do pleasing colors in the decor, without being as apparent. In a small restaurant, however, both the selection and the loudness of music call for something better than is provided by the typical background music system.

There are a number of reasons for this. Music in a restaurant serves several important functions:

- Conscious enjoyment of favorite melodies or familiar performances.
- Masking of intimate or private conversations from those at adjacent tables.
- Making an empty dining room feel less empty.
- Inducing relaxation and setting a mood consistent with the cuisine.
- Encouraging the staff to survive dull routine by providing enjoyment that does not interfere with their movements and interaction.

These functions require that the listener not have to strain to hear the music, yet not have to shout to be heard talking. Ordinary background music systems typically use few speakers, or ones with low-fidelity response. They tend to achieve a subliminal effect, whereas one of your objectives is to have your patrons remember the music along with the meal, and to recommend your restaurant because of that memory.

Choosing the music. What music do *you* like? That is as good a place to begin as any. If you serve dinner in the continental style, classical music is always appropriate. If you serve country style, bluegrass may be right. New Orleans hot jazz will do nicely for any lunch and some dinner styles. In my experience, there is no meal for which there is not some appropriate performance of one of the classics. The same may be said for other types of music, from simple folk melodies to modern jazz. The key to appropriateness is more in the number and arrangement of the instruments rather than the style of music. In both classic and contemporary music, loud brass and percussion—or any overpowering arrangement of instruments —are to be avoided; choose pieces that feature one, two, or several instruments that blend well together. A Handel recorder sonata or a Mozart quartet for flute and strings would be better than a Beethoven symphony or a Verdi opera. Violin, flute, piano, classical guitar, harp, sitar, dulcimer, harpsichord, cello, viola, French horn, oboe, recorder, even the electronic organ, can all be pleasing alone or in combination. The voice is a very appropriate instrument for restaurant music, provided the lyrics are right and the accompaniment meets the above criteria for restraint and peacefulness.

Aiming for excellence in music is likely to pay off as well as it does in food. So when that big guy with the "savage breast" comes in, what are you going to soothe it with? Quiche Lorraine? Yes, but also maybe Alfred Brendel or Maria Muldaur, Vladimir Horowitz or John Denver, Yehudi Menuhin or Jean-Pierre Rampal, or all of the above plus *Eine Kleine Nachtmusik.*

The function of a restaurant and its management is simply this: to make people feel better when they leave than they did when they arrived.

How to get it. In the main, you are limited to recorded music on tape or records or radio. Some FM radio broadcasts are designed to fill restaurants' needs, along with those of office buildings, doctors' waiting rooms, beauty salons, banks, and department stores. (And maybe even used-car lots and massage parlors.) The disadvantages of FM broadcasts are obvious. You lack choice, except for choice of station. Some stations have good music, but also broadcast news, commercials, or other features inappropriate for your restaurant. The automated stations with few commercials often play what my son Michael calls "laxative music." (In the trade, such stations are actually known as Beautiful Music, or B.M., stations.) One of the less obvious disadvantages is that for several weeks before Christmas these stations may play hours and hours of carols, until you're ready to commit mayhem on some unsuspecting Santa Claus.

The advantage of FM music is that, if there is a station you can tolerate during all or most of your serving hours, and if you can get good reception, you can obtain the necessary FM receiver and speakers at less cost than for any other choice of system. And it will require less effort to keep your music fresh and current. To cover the times when you are not serving or when the station is not on the air, you can use an AM radio in the kitchen and some other system, such as a cassette player, in the dining room for an hour or two.

Tape systems for maximum choice. To be able to select the music to fit your mood or the customers' desires, you must install some type of recorded music system. Wider choice translates into higher cost. So does greater fidelity, stereophonic sound, and volume control in the dining room. Each of the systems discussed below has inherent disadvantages in installation, operation, and availability of specific music. Also, under the 1976 copyright law and a 1982 Supreme Court decision on a clothing chain's use of tape-recorded music in retail stores, an establishment with an area of greater than 620 square feet may not play taped music on which royalties are not paid. The monthly royalty payment is not high and can be arranged through ASCAP or your audio equipment dealer.

There are available monaural systems that provide continuous music for twelve hours on a pre-recorded tape cartridge, which is very easy to insert and remove from the player. You can even select a mode that intersperses some silence in each hour of music. The player is compact enough to fit almost anywhere. This system is relatively expensive. It usually comes with one tape, with additional tapes available for a large sum. However, once you have bought that tape cartridge you have no way of recording other music over what is already on it, because the track width differs from that of most commercial or home recording equipment. You must go to the original supplier to get new music. This system offers high reliability and low maintenance; selectivity is limited, though, by the duration of the tape and the taste of the supplier. You may be able to order custom tapes made to your specifications, but the cost is likely to be exorbitant. It will be worthwhile to check with other restaurants or businesses that use such systems to see what their experience has been over a period of time. Ask a local installer of equipment to give you the names of places where he installed tape systems at least two years previously.

A cassette tape system offers a somewhat more compact player and recorder design. There is also a greater selection of recorded music available on cassettes in your area; this saves you the trouble of special ordering. Unfortunately, cassette systems suffer from a serious flaw for restaurant use: they simply require too much time and attention—for changing the tape being played—to warrant their long-term use.

So, what choice are you left with? The best alternative is a reel-to-reel tape system on which a high-fidelity stereo recording can be made and played back. Even with a seven-inch-diameter reel you will get a reasonably long playing time, if you use both the forward and reverse tracks and the slowest tape speed setting. The better reel-to-reel models offer a choice of tape speeds—seven and one-half, three and three-quarters, and one and seven-eighths inches per second—as well as an automatic reverse feature that gives you continuous repetitions of the same tape for as long as you wish. This is important when you are too busy at the moment the tape ends to set up a new reel. It also enables you to make a recording that will play back continuously for at least two hours without repeating any portion of the tape.

If you choose this type of system so that you will be able to select the particular music that best fits your restaurant, you will require a means of recording your own tapes—unless you can find pre-recorded music that meets your needs and is on the right size reel, recorded at the proper sound level. In most cases you will have to tape recordings from long-playing records, from other tapes, or from FM broadcasts. This means you must have access to at least a good stereo amplifier, a turntable, and the means to monitor your sound levels during the recording sessions (earphones, speakers, or both). The change in loudness from one selection on the tape to the next is of prime importance, since you will not have time to attend to the equipment to adjust the playback level.

Obviously, it will require many hours of painstaking effort to select, record, and replenish your library of music each year. Unless this represents a form of recreation for you or a member of your family, you may wish to delegate the task to a competent friend with good equipment in exchange for a negotiated price per tape—which could perhaps be a number of free meals.

Features to look for when purchasing a reel-to-reel tape player and recorder include:

- Capacity for at least a seven-inch-diameter reel.
- Automatic reverse.

edge of the room farthest from the performers. Naturally, your chairs must be comfortable for the duration of both the dinner and the show, which could total three or four hours.

One way to break up this period, and to solve the seating capacity problem at the same time, is to plan a short break after the dinner hour and to encourage the audience to gather in a lounge or even an outdoor patio where after-dinner drinks are served while your crew rearranges the dining room into a theater. This requires that the patrons finish their meal by the prescribed hour, but it does also allow theatergoers who do not wish to eat out to gather before curtain time. You cannot hope to fill the auditorium with dinner patrons, although if you keep the tables set up the theater-only customers who arrive early are more likely to have a drink, especially if you do not have bar service or a lounge.

The speed and efficiency with which dinner is prepared and served is a critical factor in how well you can hold the entire affair down to a reasonable duration. Some theatergoers do have to pay babysitters too. Any setup that requires the removal and replacement of seats and tables is generally an impractical use of people's energy and storage space inside the theater.

One dinner theater arrangement avoids the entire problem of food service in the theater by serving the meal first in a dining room that is connected to the theater but separated entirely from the stage area. Thus, the dinner setting can be a lovely restaurant with a charming ambience and an interesting bill of fare. The single-price dinner-theater ticket includes a choice of several regular dinner entrees at a price below what the dinner would otherwise cost if one subtracted the full price of the theater ticket. There is an entrance to the theater direct from the dining room, but theater patrons who do not wish to eat are undisturbed by last-minute clearing of food service paraphernalia. At the same time, the restaurant can continue to operate independently, both during the showtimes and when nothing at all is going on in the theater. This arrangement seems to me an excellent solution to all the difficulties presented by dinner theater.

HOW SOME OTHERS HAVE DONE IT

The three small restaurants described below are examples of what others have actually done to solve a major problem of location, remodeling, or aptness of style for the premises. They are quite different kinds of places, but they all reflect some common characteristics. They are the unique expressions of their founders' individual styles and approaches to food service. Each is comfortable in terms of friendliness and concern for the patrons, though not all exhibit sophisticated taste in decor. They also share an enviable reputation for excellence. The different owners are alike in that none is likely to do what others want; rather, each will do precisely what he or she believes strongly in. It is not surprising that the result is uncompromising high quality, uniqueness, customer and critical acclaim, and financial success.

SHIRO—An ethnic restaurant in an unlikely spot. A Japanese restaurant out in the middle of nowhere, forty miles from Boston? How did it ever get there? *Shiro* means castle in Japanese, and for Mrs. Yoshiko Sefton, a Japanese war bride, her castle was born of necessity. When her American-born husband died several years ago, she and her children were without support, but not without ingenuity, courage, and determination. Yoshiko Sefton is a woman who knows what she wants and goes after it. Dauntless and independent, she does not ask others for too much advice.

In 1976, Mrs. Sefton was approached by a young Japanese chef who wanted to leave a Boston restaurant but had nowhere to go except back to Japan. Seizing this opportunity, Mrs. Sefton found a location that was right near her own town and ideally suited to her needs. The older three-story house had already been converted to a conventional restaurant, including a small bar. Even after the installation of an open cooking area behind a low counter suitable for sushi service in part of the former dining room, there was still room for about fifteen tables in the remaining rooms. Shiro opened in June 1976, after only one month's work to convert the layout to suit Japanese cooking.

The restaurant is remotely located in the small town of Berlin, Massachusetts (population 2,300) on Route 62. But its remoteness is mitigated by its proximity to an exit from Interstate Route 495, a major highway that links southern and northern New England. Shiro's clientele consists of a varied mix of businesspeople, local residents, travelers, and military personnel (especially those with Oriental spouses) based at Fort Devens, about twenty-five minutes away. It helps, of course, that there are no other Japanese restaurants within at least twenty-five miles.

The main problems facing Mrs. Sefton now are those of supply. Fresh fish for her sashimi and yakizakana dishes is becoming scarcer, and for this reason she serves the full sushi menu only on Wednesdays. Most of her staple supplies are delivered from New York City by vendors of Oriental foods. In this respect also, it is Shiro's easy access from the interstate highway, combined with an increase of interest in Japanese cooking in this country, that makes business at that location viable.

THE HAMLET—Converting an abandoned building. The health inspector said it couldn't be done. But Norm and Maggie Hamlet of Los Angeles and Cambria, California were convinced that the location for their small Armenian-style restaurant in Harmony, California (population 18) was feasible. No matter that the old Harmony Valley Creamery Association building was hardly a building at all anymore, especially the shed-like structure that would become their dining room. It was the proposed kitchen area that the inspector had vetoed.

Norm insisted on knowing what requirements they had to meet, and explained to the inspector how they would construct a "building within a building" to satisfy all the codes. And so they did. The Hamlets negotiated a five-year lease for the restaurant space, with an option to renew for another five years. They paid for all the remodeling, but much of the actual work was done by the owner of the building and by the Hamlets themselves. Building permits were originally applied for in 1974; but delays, red tape, and slow construction prevented completion of the work until May 1975, when "The Hamlet" restaurant opened as the main attraction in a collection of small artisans' shops.

Within a few months the Hamlet had attracted loyal customers and critical acclaim for its food, decor, and friendly atmosphere. The dining room combined authentic weathered wood with the freshness of flowers and crisp blue linen. Despite the limitations of their tiny kitchen and storage spaces, on a busy night four to five times the population of Harmony was served at the ten tables of the Hamlet.

The restaurant, though successful, eventually moved to a new location for a variety of reasons. Tiny Harmony is located on California's foggy coastal Route 1 north of Morro Bay, in an area most heavily traveled during the summer by people heading for the Hearst Castle at San Simeon or points north on the scenic highway leading to Big Sur and the Carmel-Monterey peninsula. In 1977, a new owner took over the Harmony real property, and differences arose between the new landlord and the Hamlets. The restaurateurs were also suffering from the effects of an exhausting schedule of lunch and dinner service and from their space limitations. Just after the Memorial Day weekend in 1978, the Hamlet restaurant in Harmony closed. The remaining time on the lease as well as the furniture, fixtures, and decor were sold to the new landlord.

The Hamlet was relocated in a newly constructed adjunct to a two-year-old motel on a highway frontage road just south of the Hearst Castle State Historical Monument in San Simeon, which is visited each year by nearly one million people. These more spacious and practical quarters offered the possibility to improve the kitchen design and to expand the dining room capacity, yet keep the character of a small restaurant with closely controlled quality. But the ultimate effect of the move remains to be seen. The restaurant was not reopened until mid-July, missing nearly half of the summer season while final work was being done on the building. Some old customers were lost through a combination of an inflation-induced rise in prices and the added distance for the established clientele to reach the new location. Nevertheless, the potential for good patronage can be realized, if the coastal weather and general economic conditions remain relatively clear. Persistence and maintenance of the fine, friendly dining experience at the Hamlet should overcome the effects of uprooting an established business with an excellent reputation.

BECKOLA—Food service from a downtown cranny. When Beca Poe used to walk past the little hole-in-the-wall place on Monterey Street in San Luis Obispo, California where dehydrated food and other sundries were on sale, she often wondered why anyone ever went in there. She never did, until one hot day when she wanted something healthful to drink, and realized she might find it in there. "This place is for sale," the proprietor said after talking for a while to Beca, "and I want you to buy it." Before the day was over, Beca had bought the stock plus a lease on the entire store space—only 200 square feet!

Beckola hardly qualifies as a restaurant, per se. The menu offers juices and smoothies, and a variety of hot and cold natural food prepared without refined sugar, white flour, or chemical additives or preservatives. Although much of the food is served on a take-out basis, there are seats for seven patrons at three tables. And all the food is prepared on the premises, if a kitchen area of about eight by ten feet can be called a premises. Beca's previous experience as manager of a natural foods restaurant was the basis for her present venture.

With the help of her partner, artist and designer Dennis "Woody" Combrink, and of friends who fabricate equipment and furniture from wood and steel, a special set of counters and other furnishings was designed and built to provide flexibility and mobility in the cramped space. Anything that must be moved to allow supplies to be brought in is on wheels. All the health codes are met, including the requirement for a bathroom, which sometimes serves as a temporary storage room.

Beckola is open from 11 a.m. to 9 p.m. Monday through Saturday. The clientele includes local businesspeople as well as many of the students attending nearby California Polytechnic University. And people come in from the surrounding communities to shop in the downtown business district of San Luis Obispo; many of them stop at Beckola while in town.

Beckola does not have much conventional restaurant equipment; there is no stove, for example. There is no need for a hood, since the soup du jour is made in an electric crock pot, and the rice in an electric rice steamer. There are juicers of all sorts, blenders in great abundance, and a special piece of equipment that washes great quantities of vegetables and fruit. Dishwashing is avoided by serving food on wicker trays lined with wax paper. Liquids are served in disposable containers. There is a sink, as well as some refrigeration. And, except for chronic claustrophobia, it works. I'm not certain, but I am willing to bet that Beckola is the smallest restaurant in the country with original paintings on the walls, excellent food, and a very determined woman behind a portable counter.

6. Dining Room Practice

RESTAURANT is theater. If you view your dining room operation with this perspective, you will work from the right starting point. From the moment the customers first make contact with the players—whether this is on the telephone, in person, or even by letter—the tone of the response they get is essential to their dining pleasure. As in theater, both the voice and the body must convey your message. The message a small restaurant gives is friendship, calm and graceful service, and artfully prepared food of the highest quality. The mood and demeanor of the dining room staff bespeaks this message in the subtlest ways.

> *Everyone who answers the telephone at your restaurant should be trained to use a pleasant, well-modulated voice. The opening phrase should be "Good morning [afternoon, evening]," followed by the name of the restaurant. You can check on how well it is done by calling your place at different times.*

Whether your show is just a little "one-act" breakfast or lunch stop, an "improvisational" buffet restaurant, or a "grand opera" dinner house complete with curtain calls by the chef after the final act, it will follow certain basic and logical sequences intended to please the audience and ensure smooth timing of the performance. The following synopsis of restaurant scenes describes dinner in a typical "three-act" table-service establishment. With some additions or deletions, it applies as well to the service of other meals or to variants of the table-service restaurant. It should establish a framework on which to build an understanding of the specific topics discussed in detail in this and subsequent chapters.

BEFORE THE SHOW

On Stage

• The servers arrive early enough to check and fill all dispensers of condiments, relish, beverages, salad bins, ice, water, linen, silverware, and so on. Tables are set, menus and "specials" are noted, and wine lists reviewed.

• The host, maitre d', or captain checks reservations; plans for large parties that will require moving of tables; checks dining room temperature and lighting, rest room conditions and supplies; and double checks on the preparations of servers and buspersons, especially the initial setup of tables and serving stations. Candles or table lights and flowers are checked and replenished, if needed. Just before opening, the dining room floor and seats are scrutinized for hazards, debris, or water.

• The manager and chef give last-minute instructions for handling specific parties, and on how to describe the ingredients

Backstage

• The chef and kitchen personnel have prepared any foods whose cooking time began before opening. Backup amounts for service later in the evening are in preparation. For dishes that are prepared to order, setup is made for ease of continuous operations during the mealtime. Extra salad and dressings are made ready; vegetables and garnishes are pre-sliced; and cuts of meat or seafood are prepared and trimmed based on the number of reservations and anticipated business for the meal to come. Ovens and steam table are prepared for use.

• The dishwasher stacks clean plates where the chef can easily get to them for meal assembly. The dishroom is cleaned up from washing the prep utensils, and bus trays and carts are wiped clean in readiness for dining room dishes. Bins for dirty linen, trash, bottles, and garbage are emptied. The dish-

On Stage (continued)

and preparation of special dishes or sauces for that night. Any regular items in short supply are discussed; and hints for promoting fresh items or special desserts that might spoil are suggested, especially if it is the night before the restaurant is normally closed.

• If server rotation or table stations are not already assigned, they are now clearly established. Note is taken of any servers who are scheduled to arrive after the start of the serving to handle the busiest hours, and any who are scheduled to depart early are so reminded. New employees are reminded about important procedures and the handling of tips.

• Outside signs and lights are checked, if necessary.

Backstage (continued)

washing machine is checked for wash and rinse water temperature.

• The servers set up plates, utensils, and supplies for any items that they normally assemble and serve, such as salads, soup, desserts, butter, relish, crackers, bread sticks, hot bread or rolls, house wines, and side orders.

• The refrigerator stocks are checked for items regularly dispensed, such as drinks and special condiments for that meal. Backup stocks in the storeroom or cooler are also checked to ensure replenishment of the reach-in refrigerators.

• The chef gives last-minute instructions to the host or maitre d' and the servers about any important changes in menu, routine, or timing to accommodate the night's menu or the state of readiness in the kitchen.

• Sometimes staff meals are served before the start of the dinner hour. This is not the usual practice for servers, but is more common for dishwashers.

WHEN THE CURTAIN RISES

On Stage

• The host seats the diners. After taking care of coats, the host or another staff member offers the menu and wine list. Special items are announced or regrets expressed for any items that are all gone. Often the server's name in announced at the table.

• The server acknowledges the party's presence and arrives as soon as practical to take orders. Sufficient time is allowed for diners to study the menu. Relish, water, and whatever else is served early are delivered to the table.

• Orders for aperitifs, cocktails, and other beverages are taken and served according to your custom. At the right moment, according to the diners' wishes and your custom, the food order and dinner wine order are taken. For large parties or unusual requests the server notes carefully the seating arrangement and sequence of the orders taken. Often for very large parties more than one server takes orders, with the group split up in a logical way. Even if this is not done, a large party is usually served the hot food by more than one server. If separate checks are allowed for large groups, the server arranges for it in advance of order taking.

Backstage

• According to the established kitchen practice, the server delivers the order ticket to the chef, often accompanied by a verbal announcement ("Order!"), especially when the chef is not at his usual station. The server carefully notes which parts of the order he or she must prepare or assemble (such as different salad dressings and beverages) and the proper timing for each. Any special instructions to the chef or variations requested by the diner are noted plainly on the order ticket, and also are usually pointed out verbally at the time the ticket is turned in.

• If responsibility for taking the orders for drinks and serving them does not lie with the regular server, the necessary coordination of service and tallying the price on the order or dinner check is arranged between the people involved.

• According to your kitchen practice, early courses such as soup and salad are assembled either by the server, by kitchen assistants, or by both, for each table.

• Supplies of hot bread, rolls, or other side dishes served from the kitchen are kept at a level sufficient to serve the number of diners out front.

On Stage (continued)

• Early courses are served without interfering with aperitifs or before-meal wines. Dirty dishes from the preceding course are always removed before serving the next course. Any untouched plate of food must be noted by the server, who is on the alert for something amiss. Whatever course immediately precedes the main dish (usually it's salad) is carefully watched for completion so that it may be removed or set to the side to allow service of the hot main course as soon as it is ready.

• When the main dish has been at the table for one or two minutes, the server returns to ask if all is well and if any last-minute requests can be filled.

Backstage (continued)

• The buspersons apprise the servers and chef of the progress of clearing early course plates from each table, to ensure timely serving of the next course.

• The chef looks at the main course orders for that table and mentally notes the required cooking time for each order so that the diners in that group can be served all at the same time. When the server later signals that the course before the entree has been served, the chef starts that table's orders, if possible. On nights when time permits it, the chef often will ask to be told about slow eaters so as to avoid rushing them.

• The warm plates are set up for assembly of the meal, and the dinner items are artfully arranged to make an attractive and appetizing array with the garnishes and any special side condiments. At the right time during this assembly, the server is signaled for pickup.

• The server appears to pick up the order just as the last plate is being finished (for large parties, the last plate the server can carry at one time). The server always checks the order ticket before taking the plates; any errors are corrected quickly. The plates are taken up so that the ladies at the table are the first to be served (eldest first), except that when

On Stage (continued)

• Servers and buspersons are on the alert throughout the meal to anticipate the need for more bread, rolls, butter, cream, coffee, tea, or water, or for other such requests; and to provide assistance with spills or other mishaps, especially when there are small children present.

• When the diners are obviously finished with the main course, the plates have been removed, and dessert is still to be ordered, the server reappears for that purpose. Otherwise, the dessert is announced and served, along with any other last courses such as fruit and cheese, coffee, tea, after-dinner wines, or whatever.

• The dinner check is not tallied until it is reasonably certain that the diners' wants have been fully satisfied. If it is your custom not to present the check until it is requested, be sure the customer is aware of that. Large party checks are reviewed for arithmetic errors or omissions by a second person before they are presented to the table. (This is a good practice for all checks, if time permits.)

• Your policy on personal checks and credit cards may be discussed when the check is presented. If the diner is expected to make payment to a cashier, that fact must be made clear as well.

Backstage (continued)

the far side of the table is difficult to reach those seated on that side, male or female, are served first. Meat entrees that have been cooked to order (rare, medium, well-done, or gradations thereof) are identified to the server for proper delivery at the table.

• Whenever possible, everything that can be done to anticipate the chef's next need—whether for plates, utensils, or components of the meal being assembled—is done by those assisting the chef. All spills are immediately wiped away to avoid accidents, staining, or burns to the server or the diner. Plates with hot food are not overfilled for the same reason.

On Stage (continued)

• When the server, the host, or the manager handles a credit card payment or returns change and receipt for a cash transaction, the guests are thanked and asked to comment on the restaurant or to recommend it to friends. This can also take place when coats are returned or the guest book is signed.

• As soon as the party leaves the table, any dirty plates, glasses, silverware, and other remnants of the meal are quietly removed by using some type of tray or bus container. Depending on your custom, either the server, the busperson, or the host takes care to remove the tip, if it was left in cash on the table. The table and the area around it are examined for articles that may have been dropped or forgotten by the diners, so that they may be returned before the people have left the restaurant.

• The empty table and the floor are checked for spills and food particles, and the table is reset using a clean cloth if necessary. It is set for the exact number in the party awaiting that table; otherwise it is set for whatever number is practical. Toward the end of the mealtime vacated tables often are not reset or are reset for the next mealtime, when tableware settings will be different.

Backstage (continued)

• The dirty dishes, tableware, and linens from the dining room are delivered directly to the dishroom, never near the area where food is being prepared or meals assembled. Whenever possible, kitchen personnel assist servers whose orders are waiting for pickup by taking dirty dishes from them so the servers can proceed directly to the pickup upon entering the kitchen. The dishwasher facilitates deposit of dirty dishes by keeping the dishroom free of spills or tall stacks of dishes in or near the repository for dirty tableware, and by making available an empty bin or other area that the server or busperson can reach without bending down. The buspersons assist in this during the busiest times by holding dirty dishes in the dining room or other places, so long as the tables are cleared as quickly as needed.

• The chef must first be consulted about any requests from diners to give compliments in person to the chef, or to enter the kitchen area for any reason whatsoever.

AFTER CURTAIN CALLS

On Stage

• The night's receipts are counted by the manager and the dinner checks totaled. Tips that were included on credit card drafts are paid in cash to the servers. At the same time the checks are reviewed for errors in prices charged, and for items that were served but omitted from the check. Errors are discussed with the servers, especially those in training, either that same evening or the next day.

• The dining room is cleaned to remove food particles and the remains of spills. Salt, pepper, and sugar holders are carefully wiped clean of food residues and are refilled for the next mealtime. Depending on your custom, tables are set for the next meal service or wiped clean and prepared for the next crew to set them up.

• The rest rooms are thoroughly cleaned and supplies replenished.

• The windows and doors are closed and locked and any alarms for smoke or burglary detection are set. Air conditioning, fans, and heating units are turned off.

• Music equipment is prepared for the next day's use and turned off.

Backstage

• The crew is served whatever meals you customarily serve. The cleanup crew begins work on the kitchen as soon as possible after the food is put away. The servers and kitchen assistants complete their sidework chores and replenish supplies.

• All usable leftovers are placed in tightly covered containers with as little room for air as possible. Perishable food and supplies are returned quickly to the refrigerators and cooler. The chef decides what use may be made of leftovers for the next day's specials for lunch or dinner. Notes are written for the early morning cooks, giving important instructions about use of leftovers, deliveries of supplies, or other ideas not part of the routine.

• The cleanup crew takes apart the steam table and all food-processing equipment, such as slicers, and puts parts that touch the food directly through the dishwasher or disinfectant, while wiping down the rest of the equipment. The stove, griddle, grill, and microwave ovens receive special attention in the cleanup. Usually, the food preparation areas in which servers have done their work are wiped

On Stage (continued)

- Unnecessary inside lights are turned off or dimmed. Outside lights or lighted signs are turned off if not on a timer.

- The sign is turned to "closed."

Backstage (continued)

clean by the servers before they depart, as are the coffee maker and milk dispenser. The cleanup crew double checks these areas. The floor is swept and mopped clean each night.

- The dishwasher completes his chores: puts away all dishware, glassware, and tableware; scours all the pots; and cleans and rinses away all food particles in and around the dishwashing machine and drainboards. The machine is turned off and the tank drained (be sure that the heater is off). Walls around the dishroom are wiped down.

- All garbage, trash, empty bottles, and other disposables are removed from the kitchen area to whatever outdoor or enclosed place is available.

- The closing security checklist is followed for turning off ovens, steam table, other heating elements, fans, and lights. Storeroom locks are checked, as are the windows and doors to the kitchen.

RESERVATIONS

"No one will be seated after curtain time." In a small restaurant, "curtain time" for a table on a busy night is the time reserved. If you take reservations, do not hold them for more than a few minutes when someone else is waiting for a table. Tell callers when you accept their reservation how long it will be held on a busy night.

Scheduling table use. When scheduling reservations, how long do you figure a table will be occupied by one party? This is determined by several factors, including the number of courses in the meal, the number of tables the server must take care of, the speed and coordination in the kitchen, and whether you serve wine and desserts. There are ι few other minor factors whose influence is subtle—the hardness of the seat, the temperature of the room, the proximity of the restaurant to another attraction such as a theater, and even whether the waiting room full of people can be seen by those still at table. The range of occupancy time for planning optimum table use is from about one hour per party to as long as one and three-quarters hours. If someone lingers for more than that and you need the table, you are in trouble.

If your meals are long affairs, you will have to have more tables or higher prices, or both, to make up for the loss of turnover. You may even choose to have only two seatings per night and to fill up twice by reservation only. This is practical only when your reputation and the demand for your services permit you to limit flexibility. There are restaurants in California, though, whose waiting lists for such seating are six weeks long.

Simultaneous seating. Do not hesitate to tell someone requesting a reservation that the time he desires is not convenient but that you will have a table fifteen minutes earlier or later. He will usually take it, and this device smoothes the flow of parties. In a small dining room with only two or three servers, it is not a good idea to have a lot of parties seated all at once. The exception to this rule is at opening time, when it is not so bad.

Spacing the parties by five to fifteen minutes also improves the work flow in the kitchen. If you have a limited amount of any special entree on the menu for the evening, it is important to be able to notify people as they are seated that the special is all gone. If they were seated at about the same time as three other parties, they will resent being left out. In addition, having a few minutes between seatings gives the servers time to take orders in a systematic manner.

When a time period for dining room use is already booked for all your tables, it is sometimes still possible to squeeze in one more party. Make a note on your reservation sheet whenever a party has arrived and been seated early. Also check the progress at the tables to see if there are any fast eaters who may not have dessert or coffee. You may be able to feed a hungry family who just found your place by accident and had no time to reserve a table.

"No-shows." If you clearly explain that you will not hold reservations for more than five minutes, ninety-nine out of a hundred people will understand why you gave away their table when they were late. Of course, the other one in a hundred may be like the party of six that reserved a table at our restaurant for 8 p.m. on Friday and did not show up. The next night, when we were completely booked up for the evening, the previous night's no-shows appeared at 8 p.m. with sheepish grins. Some people will try anything once.

Especially on busy nights, it is a good rule to give away a table to a waiting party if the one with the reservation does not show up within a few minutes of the appointed time. The exception is for a large party. It always takes a little longer for a large group to get going, so they are often late. Unless you have several large tables available, you should give them ten to fifteen minutes to arrive. More often than not, they will show up. Just hope they don't appear just after you have given their table to a party of two.

Once upon a time there was a man named Williams who made a reservation at a small restaurant for a party of twelve on a busy Saturday night. They never showed up and didn't call to cancel. Ever since then, the maitre d' gets shivers whenever anyone named Williams calls for a reservation.

Sometimes you get a feeling about whether a particular reservation will be kept. If the caller seems somehow uncertain, be sure to act on your hunch and ask him to telephone you if his plans change. (He may even do so.) Another good candidate for no-show is the party that simply must have a couple of cocktails before dinner. They show up early for that purpose, assuming you have a bar, and are chagrined to find that you serve only beer and wine. When you direct them to the nearest bar be sure to get their name, so you can call to find out if they are still there when they fail to arrive for their reserved table. It may not affect you the same way, but I always felt downright insulted when someone didn't show up for a reservation and didn't call to cancel. Those who did call, whatever the stated reason, received our warmest thanks and our sincere hope to serve them some other time.

GREETING PATRONS

The front desk host, hostess, maitre d', or owner sets the scene as narrator of your restaurant "play." He also doubles as usher, ticket seller, and supporting character. Before long, this versatile member of the cast will be able to discern in a second or two whether the people who enter are intent on dining or have just stopped by to see what your place is like. During those first few seconds, the potential customer gets a feeling of welcome or indifference, a sense of quality and price, and a desire either to stay or to leave gracefully. Some will say, "We'll be back." Nothing gave me more satisfaction than when, on certain slow evenings, people stopped in to the restaurant because it "looked interesting," perused the menu, asked how long before they could have a table, and then went to check out another nearby restaurant. In four or five minutes they would reappear for a table. Invariably, they said they had returned "because this place smelled great and looked so nice and homey." But it is more than decor or aroma. The feeling of a dining room also depends on the subtle messages that emanate from the people who manage it.

It should be a firm requirement that every member of the staff in the dining room be prepared to give a friendly greeting to customers who enter the restaurant. Whoever notices them first should make eye contact and say something with a smile. If the host or maitre d' is occupied elsewhere at the moment, the greeting should be issued by a server, a busperson, or even by the dishwasher who happens to be there picking up a tray full of dirty dishes. There is something special about being noticed and acknowledged immediately. Seeds of uncertainty are planted in every minute that one is ignored, especially if the staff is scurrying about. It is as if the curtain has gone up on the first act, but all you see are stagehands acting as if the curtain were still closed.

"Watch the coats." I never believed that those "watch your coat" signs in coffee shops were really necessary until I became responsible for everyone's coats. The problem of checking coats and hats is not a trivial one, especially in areas where cold winters call for expensive garments like goose-down jackets. Hang coats where they can be watched carefully by either the cashier or the patrons. Expensive raincoats, hats, and favorite garments do get deliberately or accidentally taken. If you allow people to keep their wraps at the table, be particularly careful when serving boiled potatoes and beet borscht.

King Vidor, the film director, was an occasional but devoted patron of our restaurant. One day he left his hat on the antique English bentwood hall tree, and forgot it when he departed. When he got home, he called to assure himself that I had his favorite hat, a beautiful old wide-brimmed felt work of the highest quality. I promised to guard it well. But there really was no good place to keep the hat where it would have proper protection, yet be visible to one of our staff in case Mr. Vidor should come for it while I was gone. Finally I decided to put it in a conspicuous but safe place. At the time, our bubble-top dessert cart was not being used and was kept in the entry room. I placed Mr. Vidor's hat inside it on a napkin. It attracted much comment, especially from those who thought it was a marvelously crafted cake; but those to whom I revealed that it was King Vidor's hat thought me daft.

If you have to make a party wait quite a while in your waiting room, offer them a complimentary aperitif or glass of wine to help them relax. Have one yourself on a crazy, busy night.

SERVER STATIONS

The routine for assigning tables is designed with one main purpose: to provide the best possible timing for meal service by balancing the load on each server and busperson. Each table in the dining room should be given a number; a chart of the dining room layout should be posted in the kitchen for easy reference by the staff. Some restaurants then establish a fixed "station," or area of tables, to be each server's responsibility. As they arrive, customers are directed by the host to tables in each station in rotation. The only foul-up in the plan occurs when the customer insists on sitting at a table out of rotation sequence, which can temporarily overload one server while another is idle.

Another method that works in a small dining room is to allow the servers to take parties in rotation as they arrive, regardless of table. This can also cause an overload, though, if chance causes the larger parties all to fall to one server for several rounds. But a balance can easily be worked out by switching parties, especially if reservations allow some advance planning.

Most servers view table assignment as a means of ensuring that they all get a fair share of the tips. When an inexperienced server has just started work, however, it is important to limit the number of tables he or she is assigned, in order to give the newcomer time to learn the job well. But the question of tips is not a simple one. If you want to see the preliminaries to a cat fight, just listen to the reaction of other servers to one who grabs too many parties in a rotation system. Not only does this situation cost the other servers some tips, but it usually costs your patrons some comfort as well, when they sense the friction between the staff members or are badly served by the overloaded one. You must watch for and prevent such back-biting.

There is a lot to be said for having all servers pool their tips for the shift, as a way of defusing pettiness. In order for this system to work well, the servers must feel that each is doing a fair share of the sidework and setup, cleanup, and preparation for the next shift. This can easily be accomplished if all the people make an effort to get along. Pooling tips has the added advantage of making it easier to decide who should be assigned which station or parties. It also diminishes the effect on one server of getting a small tip, or getting "stiffed" (no tip). Pooling tips does require that your servers all be of approximately equal skill, so that no one is constantly asking for help from the others.

Why should a server get "bummed out" by an occasional small tip when he or she has given good service? The same service to another customer will elicit a very large tip on another occasion. As with other things in life, it all averages out.

WHAT HAPPENS AT THE TABLE

Menu and wine list. Your customer has been comfortably seated, coats and hats have been accounted for, and the menu and wine list offered. At this point it is imperative that the server for that table acknowledge the diners' presence as soon as possible. If the server cannot approach the table within a reasonably short time, it is still possible for the customer to be reassured by a nod, a smile, or preferably a few words saying that she will be with them momentarily. One way of doing this is to deliver a small relish dish or appetizer for them to munch on while they decide what to order.

Some restaurants do not have the wine steward or server ask about interest in wine until the dinner has been ordered. I find this an unnecessary and sometimes annoying delay. People are entitled to decide for themselves, in whatever order they choose, whether or not to have wine. The menu and wine list should be presented at the start, when the party is seated. However, because there are some nondrinkers who act offended if wine is offered, be certain to inquire first if the wine list is of interest to them. (Thank goodness for the many people who would be offended if the wine list were not offered.)

It is more efficient if all your servers are thoroughly familiar with your wine list and with any selections that are not listed. But at dinner time, when the servers must respond promptly to the demands of kitchen and patrons, it is important to have someone else available in the dining room who can knowledgeably discuss and recommend wines to your guests. There are more and more Americans now who are drinking fine wines, and they like to try something new on a night out. Even Sylvia Porter is writing columns for the consumer on purchasing wine for home entertaining. If you do not yet have a good knowledge of wine, make the next book you read one on that subject. Soon you'll know *Vitis vinifera* from *Vitis labrusca,* dry from sweet, and varietals from all over. The stocking of wines is discussed in Chapter 7.

Taking the order. There are several ways to handle the order taking. Most restaurants today use either a single guest check or one that is prepared in duplicate. If you keep your alcoholic beverage records separate, you may, in addition, use a separate bar check. The advantage of a two-part guest check is that while the chef works from one copy, the server can refer to the other for preparing drinks, serving the correct salad dressing, and recalling special instructions. If a single check is used, the server must either remember everything well or constantly refer to the order wheel. Of course, in the good old days, everyone was expected to remember everything and nothing was written down. That kind of server and chef is an endangered species. But they provide a goal to strive for. Don't ever let anyone tell you that being a waitress or a waiter is for dummies. To be an excellent one requires the highest intelligence and sensitivity.

One of the nicest phrases on a menu is this: "Whenever possible, we will be happy to accommodate your special taste or dietary need." The management can decide whether "whenever possible" is now, but it is usually easy to accommodate those people who cannot eat this or that.

Special orders. Do not permit your customers to reserve one of your special menu items for the time they plan to arrive. If you run out of the special before they get there, you run out. There is nothing more annoying to your other customers than to be told that the special is gone, only to see it served half an hour later to people who were seated after them. This would not apply to special items, not on the menu, that have been pre-arranged between the patron and the chef.

Serving the wine. There is no great mystery to traditional wine service at the table. If you are serving a good selection of California wines the quality of one year's vintage will not vary much from another year's. Therefore, the traditional tasting ritual has just one important purpose: to determine whether the particular bottle being served has kept well. If a dry or faulty cork has allowed air to oxidize (maderize) the wine, or to cause it to turn sour, these faults will be discernible by sight and smell, as well as by taste. The tasting ritual is designed to avoid serving the customer a bad wine. The routine is simple and logical:

- Deliver the wine to the table as soon as possible after it is ordered.
- The opening and tasting should take place before food is served so the diner has a clear palate. Red wine should be opened and given time to "breathe" before it is drunk.
- White and rose wine should be served chilled, but not so cold that the fruity bouquet is dulled.

- Red wine should be served at room temperature, which means about 60° F (room temperature before central heating was invented).
- Always show the label to allow the customer to verify the wine selection and vintage, if any. I recommend that the server quietly mention the basic data, saying something like, "Full bottle of Fortino Petite Syrah, 1975, for you, madame."
- Red wine, especially, should not be jostled, so that any sediment remains at the bottom of the bottle.
- The lead foil cover must be cut well below the lip of the bottle to ensure that no taste of lead is imparted to the wine. The occasional residue and mold uncovered at the top of the cork and bottle lip should be carefully wiped away. The recent use of various plastic foil covers with perforations already built in allows easy removal.
- The wine glasses should be of clear glass, with a capacity of about eight to ten ounces.
- Smelling the cork is the first way to detect any potential problem. It should smell of wine, not corky or musty. The server should smell it, if it seems inappropriate to remove the cork from the corkscrew and hand it to the person who ordered the wine. The use of a two-pronged waiter's cork remover/recorker will reduce the time needed for this part of the ritual. An excellent all-metal version is marketed under the name "Ah So." (The one with the plastic handle or sheath doesn't last in restaurant use.)
- A small amount of wine is poured into the glass of the person who ordered the wine. Tip the top of the bottle close to the glass, and finish the maneuver by gently resting the neck of the bottle on the edge of the glass and twisting the bottle a quarter turn as the tip is lifted. This will halt the flow without having any wine run down the neck of the bottle.
- Wait patiently while the wine is swirled around the glass to release more wine molecules into the air in the glass, which is then held up to the nose so the bouquet can be noted. The color and clarity of the wine will also be examined against a source of light.
- When the wine is tasted and found to be sound, pour not more than half a glassful for each of the rest of the party,

usually starting with the women at the table, before returning to finish filling the glass of the taster.
- Place the bottle on the table where the host of the party can easily reach it.

House or bar wine, served from an open bottle or decanter, is not subject to the tasting ritual, for obvious reasons.

The service of champagne (or sparkling wine) can be dangerous if not done with caution. Champagne should be more chilled than white still wine, to about 40° F. The bottle should be carefully brought to the table in an ice bucket large enough to keep the whole bottle chilled through a leisurely dinner. After verification of the label, return the bottle to the bucket and remove the wire hood by placing the thumb of one hand over the top of the cork; the wire loop is held firmly with the other hand while it is worked up and down rapidly until the wire breaks. The cork may then be removed by grasping it firmly between the thumb and forefinger and rocking it back and forth as it is pulled carefully out of the bottle. The carbonation pressure of the champagne will sometimes shoot the cork out at a very high speed—sufficient to cause an eye injury or break an overhead light fixture. Therefore, an inexperienced server should first drape a clean napkin over the top of the bottle, and then remove the wire hood and cork under its protection. If the bottle is properly chilled and has not been jostled, the wine should not bubble out. If the cork is held very close to the top of the bottle upon removal, it can sometimes prevent spilling of the wine while allowing enough gas to escape to relieve the pressure.

Enforcing alcoholic beverage control laws. For a restaurant serving fermented spirits but no hard liquor, the requirement to prevent underage persons from imbibing can be an annoying one to comply with. In most states the failure to do so can cost both the server and licensee a lot of money. Check with your local bluenoses to see how they expect you to do it, so that in the case where you are fooled by a forged I.D. you will be off the hook. The only pleasant part of the whole process is that you have the chance to make some over-thirty woman feel good by asking for her I.D. But do so with caution; there should be at least a doubt.

"How is everything?" Within a few minutes after delivery of the main course, the server should return to the table to ask this question. Even if there are no complaints, this creates the feeling that the management cares about whether the food is being enjoyed. It also provides an opportunity for the server to check on the need for more water, butter, bread, or wine. The diners also have the chance to ask for anything extra they may have neglected to order.

Desserts. The difference between just having a reputation for good food and getting rave reviews may hinge on whether or not you offer special desserts. Homemade desserts are the denouement, the major scene of Act III. If your dessert offerings don't vary much from day to day, it may be best to put them on the menu. However, the way your servers describe the desserts can mean the difference between a customer ordering or passing up the final course.

You may prefer to include dessert in the dinner price, but that is not really fair to those who never eat desserts. The dessert portions need not be large; they are worth a fair price even for a small after-dinner size.

You may find people ordering a dessert item they have enjoyed at lunch, if you also serve that meal. Remember, on a busy dinner shift few servers are eager to make hot-fudge sundaes for a party of eight.

If you become well known for your excellent homemade desserts, you cannot afford to serve *only* dessert at night to any party, assuming yours is a small place with few tables. Once you make the rule, don't break it, even for friends.

The customer is not always right, but a complimentary dessert or an apology from the chef goes a long way toward satisfying a wrong customer.

HANDLING AN ERROR

Restaurant patrons who are somehow displeased by the food rather than by the service itself commonly conclude that they should leave a meager tip or even none. But the size of the tip should not be reduced unless they have received poor or indifferent service; diners should not vent on the server their displeasure with the kitchen. In most cases of error or dissatisfaction, the server and the management are eager to rectify it, if they are notified in time to do so. This is the reason the server or maitre d' stops at the table to ask if everything is satisfactory. That is the time for anything amiss to be reported and set right. Depending on the chef's and the management's policy, items returned to the kitchen for further cooking or because of dissatisfaction with the preparation, tenderness, or taste are usually handled on an individual basis.

It is generally only the most experienced and relaxed diners who have the self-confidence to report something amiss, especially if only one dinner out of four at the table is not right. But a sharp server can usually spot the sidelong glance between two diners, the turned-down corners of someone's mouth, and the mumbled response, "It's okay, never mind, Mildred," as sure signs of repressed distress. A gentle "Are you sure? We would like you to enjoy everything," may elicit the actual complaint. Sometimes it is simple. "My husband *hates* broccoli." Or, "This steak is really a little tough." If the management cares, something can be substituted for broccoli and perhaps another choice of entree can be allowed for the tough steak. At least a complimentary dessert or glass of wine may make everyone feel better.

The biggest favor you can do for a small restaurant owner is to recommend the place to a friend. The next biggest is to give him your honest, calm opinion about your experience at his restaurant. If you are pleased, everyone feels rewarded for their efforts. If you are dissatisfied, they can try to eliminate the problem.

One evening, a regular customer at our restaurant responded to my question about his dinner with, "The lamb is a little chewy." And I believed him when he said it tasted good and he would not like another dinner choice. But after he had paid the check and departed with his wife, I had occasion to have a slice of lamb roast for my own dinner. A little chewy, indeed! It was, for some inexplicable reason, as rubbery as an inner tube, though it did taste good. The chef had cut it with a very sharp slicing knife and had not discovered its condition. Luckily, I knew my customer's number, and I immediately phoned him to apologize. He laughed, but graciously accepted a rain check for another lamb dinner on the house, which he collected with pleasure a few weeks later. You may think it costly to respond in that way when the patron was willing to accept a little toughness in the meat. But this couple told everyone in town about how they had been treated. The good feelings engendered by such concern were worth far more to our reputation than the cost of the second dinner.

Whenever you have to deal with an unhappy customer, think about how you can convert him from a disgruntled person who may tell all his friends how much he disliked your place, into one who will tell them how well you treated him despite the problem.

Of course, the crass customer may take advantage of you. One evening when a couple complained of a tough steak *after* they had eaten all of it, their unhappiness was so believable that we subtracted the cost of the meat from the dinner price, just to be nice. After they had paid the reduced bill and left smiling, the people at the adjacent table, somewhat vexed at what they had witnessed, confided to the waitress that I had been "taken in." They said the couple had shared the steak and eaten it with gusto, exclaiming how delicious it was. So you must set a dining room policy that allows the chef to verify all complaints of toughness, lack of fresh taste or smell, or other problems.

BUSING

Busing of tables is one of the dining room procedures that reveals the basic character of a restaurant. The demand for fast clearing and resetting of tables will be highest at your peak business hours. If you do not employ buspersons, the servers will be hard pressed to do the job.

Teamwork is the key to proper busing. If each server is expected to bus the tables he serves, the routine will be less smooth than if all servers try to bus and reset any tables that become vacant. The servers must understand that making a table available for the next party is just as important as any other part of the job. The only tasks that have higher priority are delivering hot food or taking care of a spill. The entire serving and busing routine is made simpler if the servers will follow one basic rule: never leave the dining room empty-handed. If something is carried back to the dishroom on each ordinary trip, the tables will be kept relatively clear as they become available for resetting.

For busing to be done with proper form, a tray must be used to clear the dirty dishes and silverware. It should be a strict rule that glasses and cups are not to be picked up or carried by inserting the fingers into the tops. This rule is not based solely on form; it has health implications as well. Organisms from the lips of the previous customer could be transferred by the server's fingers to the next plate of food served, thence to the diner. Although this is highly unlikely, it is possible. Besides, it looks tacky. The use of a tray allows just as many glasses to be carried with style.

Noisy table clearing is both inelegant and annoying to the entire dining room. It is no more necessary to make noise when clearing a table than it is when serving it. Usually, it is the silverware that makes the most noise. If the utensils are carefully gathered and handled firmly, rather than left sprawled across the plates, they will contribute much less clatter. The main advantage to the padded dining table and tablecloth is noise reduction.

It takes extra time to replace a dirty tablecloth, but a clean cloth is more important than a little extra time. Some restaurants compromise by using a wipeable mat or cross drape on the table to cushion the plate and silverware. A paper placemat serves the same purpose, but the waste and loss of class it represents seem not worth the trouble, at least for dinner service. The only advantage to the paper placemat is that it is possible to print your menu on it; it might be a good way to handle breakfast or lunch.

When the scene is reset at the table for the next diner, the props should all be in place. As stage manager, the maitre d' should check the setting before ringing up the curtain. The bottom edges of each of the pieces of silverware should be set along an imaginary line parallel to the edge of the table. Whatever is in the center of the table—salt, pepper, and sugar dispensers at the minimum—should be wiped clean of fingerprints and neatly arranged. If there are fresh flowers on the table, as there are in most excellent restaurants, there should be no wilted ones left in the arrangement. And the "reserved seat" is worse than standing room only in the waiting room if it contains any food or beverage residue from the last performance. There are few moments more mortifying for the maitre d' than when he pulls back the chair for a lovely lady in dinner dress and discovers the lasagna sauce on the seat just as she lowers herself into it.

Food service and table busing are roles in a ballet. Coordination and smooth, quiet movements are essential. This does not mean there is no place for exuberance, humor, and natural responses to troublesome or funny situations. But loud directions or wise-guy responses must not originate with your staff. One of the unmistakable signs of a good dining room staff is that when a patron makes a request of someone other than the server assigned to his table, the request is fulfilled immediately. This kind of cooperation is also reflected in the speed and finesse with which two people clear and set a table for the next party.

DINING ROOM "NO-NO'S"

There are a few "no-no's" in a dining room. Absolutely no visible or audible anger from the staff is to be permitted in a dining room with customers in it. No loud drunks or abusive customers who are disturbing your other guests should be allowed to remain in the restaurant. The same is true for a screeching child, although occasionally the youngster can be placated with an offer of finger food, such as sliced fruit, breadsticks, raisins, or crackers; try chipped ice for the sore gums of a teething infant.

You may wish to discourage infants altogether in your place, especially if the room is really small. There have been a few times when I regretted that we provided a nice old wooden high chair. In each case, it seems obvious that the interests and comfort of the majority of your guests take precedence over the inconvenience to the parents—who should not have brought a tired, irritable child into your restaurant in the first place. You may have to suggest quietly, gently, but firmly that the child be taken out of the dining room. If there are two parents present, they can take turns caring for the infant and still get a meal eaten. If you can do so, encourage the parents by offering to keep food warm for the unlucky adult who is walking outside with the baby. Even if you do not normally serve food to go, this is one instance where you may wish to have some plastic food-to-go supplies, so that you can offer to provide the rest of the meal without suffering continued dining room disturbance. You run the risk of losing a customer; but there are a few people who are so insensitive to others in a restaurant that you are probably better off without their business anyway.

Even if you do not cater to small children by having high chairs and a children's menu, you still may not avoid an experience such as occurred at another restaurant in our town one day. It was an avant-garde, arty sort of place, whose clientele ranged from adventuresome upper-class tourists to organic health-food faddists who go to "natural" extremes. One such extremist converted her dining table to a diaper changing station for her baby, right in the middle of everyone's dinner! And the diaper was not merely wet. How would you like to have been having a $45 dinner for two at the next table?

When a customer becomes more and more demanding, impatient, and unreasonable, it is necessary for the server to become correspondingly more calm, responsive, and sweet—up to a point. When the tolerance threshhold has been passed, it is time for someone else to take over the table, so that other customers are not affected by the breach.

Customer out of control. If you serve liquor or if a customer arrives at your restaurant under the influence of alcohol, there is a chance that the drinker will get out of control. Yours is the position of authority, so do not hesitate to use it. Your other customers will appreciate and respect you for it. But proceed with caution. Your servers should be the first to alert you to a potential problem. The one serving the table should exert polite but firm pressure on the unruly customer by telling him to lower his voice and cease the disturbance, or else he will have to leave.

If you are not happy with the results, you should reinforce the message personally in a calm, steady voice, without a smile. If there seems to be someone else at the table who is more rational, or who seems upset by the boorish behavior, a quiet appeal for his assistance may help. It is fair to state that you have received a complaint about the behavior of the offender(s) at that table. (You have. The server notified you.)

Often an intoxicated party intent on making trouble will make loud complaints about the food or service or both. Your strongest urge may be to try to get them out of your place as quickly as possible, and in fact that may be the best course of action. However, you should consider this: if they entered your place heavily under the influence, and especially if you served them even one glass of wine, it is best for you and the public that they finish a meal and have some black coffee. Because if they drive off and later cause injury to anyone, including themselves or a passenger, their victims have legal recourse against you if you served the driver any alcohol. Do not hesitate, therefore, to tell someone at the table that you are concerned about their ability to drive, and insist that they have a complimentary cup of coffee.

Under no circumstances should you tolerate any verbal or physical abuse of anyone. For example, if an unruly customer touches a waitress in a way that is degrading, you should take definitive action to put a stop to it. This applies to sober as well as drunk customers.

I need not list all the circumstances that might cause you to call upon law enforcement assistance; the laws and your rights and obligations as an owner of a public restaurant are different in each state. Before you need them, you should find occasion to discuss this subject with your local police. Find out how long it will take after a phone call to have a patrol car at your front door. Discuss how best to handle a customer who is disturbing your dining room, destroying property, assaulting or battering someone, or trying to avoid payment of the bill. Follow their advice. Never use unnecessary force. You have a lot to lose if you permanently injure even a misbehaving customer. These cases are so rare in a nice small restaurant that you will probably never have to deal with them. But be prepared.

When you have had your restaurant open for two years, you will have said "thank you," in one form or another, more than 150,000 times. If you have said it much more than that, either you have a very good business or you are saying it too often.

PRESENTING THE CHECK

In the best of the old-time restaurants, the check was never presented until it was asked for. In your small place, you may not be able to wait that long, and you should find a way for the server or maitre d' to ask if the check may be presented. On especially busy nights, you will probably want to do it as soon as possible after it is determined that everything the party might desire has been offered.

The check should be delivered on a plate or tip tray. Often this is a very good time for the maitre d' to ask how the entire meal was enjoyed. Sometimes customers are confused about who will take their money—the server, the maitre d', or a cashier at the front desk. A word of explanation will help. Also, mentioning the forms of payment that are acceptable—such as credit cards, personal checks, travelers checks, currency, or barter—will help them decide.

If you accept credit cards at your place, be sure to imprint the card data legibly. Carefully note the name on the card when you return to the table for the signature on the draft. Nowadays, the card will often belong to a woman in the party, who may become annoyed if you place the draft for signature in front of her male companion.

One of the saddest events in a fine restaurant occurs when two grown people begin to argue over who will pay the check. I have seen people enter in a fine, happy mood, only to leave in a pout because of a silly argument over the check. Wise people either compromise or acquiesce graciously when confronted. But you can assist in this matter by establishing a hard and fast rule: "Whoever asks for the check first, gets it." That usually will put an end to the argument for a while.

For some parties, especially a large one or one in which both male and female guests are being entertained by a female host, you will occasionally be asked not to present the check at the table. In this case some convenient arrangement can be made, using a credit card or personal check perhaps, to pay the check afterwards. If the check is normally delivered to the table by the server, you will want to be certain to remind him of the special arrangement sometime before the end of the meal.

When you go out to dinner and you are particularly pleased by your meal (and if you can afford it), send a tip in to the chef.

Retrieving the table. One of the restaurateur's more tactful arts is getting a party that has finished dinner and paid the check to actually relinquish the table. Normally this can be accomplished by asking if more coffee is desired, or if anything else can be brought. There are also various body language signals, E.S.P. transmissions, scowls, glares, and grimaces—all designed to convey a succinct message without actually asking for the table at the risk of antagonizing a satisfied customer. The technique exists in its highest form in a small restaurant, where there are few tables and demand for them is high. When there are people with reservations waiting, and a previous party seems to think they have rented their table for the evening, each minute that the agonized host must endure takes five minutes off his life.

Do your favorite small restaurant owner a favor. If you plan to linger over dinner, either invite him sincerely to tell you when he needs the table for another party, or make reservations for a later time so that you are the last occupants of your table for the night. When the music is turned off, the lights are turned up, and the vacuum cleaner appears at the next table, you will know it is time to go home.

FOLLOW THE SCRIPT

I believe that the use of slang by a restaurant's staff can be a contributing factor to sloppiness in service. Informality and homeyness can be achieved without careless speech. Train all the "players" in your restaurant to deliver their lines professionally, usually with a smile. They sound like this:

- "Good evening. How many in your party?"
- "Your table is ready, Mr. Priapidophalus; please follow me."
- "Our special tonight is fresh Mako shark, baked to juicy perfection with herb butter and lemon wine sauce. Sheree will be right with you to take your order."
- "Hello, Mr. Priapidophalus; nice to see you tonight. I'll be right with you. Have you seen the wine list? We have a great new Sauvignon Blanc."
- "Are you ready to order? Please take your time. I'll send Daniel over to discuss the wine list. And then I'll be right back to take your order."
- "Do you prefer dry or less dry wine? Well, then I suggest a very special Sylvaner Riesling by one of our local wineries. It is the H.M.R. Franken Riesling. I'm sorry, we have that only in the full bottle. I'll bring it right away."
- "This wine is 1975 vintage and you'll note that it is estate bottled. That means that the grapes from which this wine was

made were grown in Hoffman Mountain Ranch vineyards. Will you taste, sir? Thank you. Enjoy your dinners."
- "May I take your order? How would you like your steak prepared, sir? Our house dressing is an herb-vinegar-and-oil, or you may have blue cheese, minted French, or Thousand Island. Would you like sour cream and chives with your baked potato? Tonight's fresh vegetable is steamed cauliflower with fresh Hollandaise sauce. Yes, I'll bring the sauce on the side. May I bring your soup now, or would you prefer to sip your wine for a few minutes? Thank you."
- "Our soup tonight is a homemade vegetable with leeks. I hope you enjoy it."
- "Have you finished? May I remove your plate? Thank you. Yes, the waitress will bring hot sourdough rolls with your salad in just a moment."
- "Would you like some fresh-ground black pepper on your salad? Oh, those are alfalfa sprouts. They're loaded with vitamins. You can even grow them at home."
- "Would you like to keep your salad? Your entree will be served in just a moment."
- "Medium-rare sirloin steak for you, sir, and medium for you, sir."
- "Are your dinners all right here, gentlemen?"
- "Would you like to have one of our homemade desserts tonight?"
- "We have a variety of teas available. Would you like lemon with your tea?"
- "Is there anything else I may bring for you?"
- "I'm glad you enjoyed your dinners tonight. May I bring your check?"
- "Here is your change for fifty dollars, and your receipt. Thank you."

Find occasion to listen to the way each server describes your menu items and the methods of preparation. A good server will find a choice of words that enhances the description by making it sound as appetizing as possible. If an item is baked or broiled, it should be described as coming out "moist" or "juicy"—if it is in fact served that way. It is better to say "juicy" than "not dry," and "sauteed in butter" rather than "pan fried." Say "prepared to your order" rather than "cooked here." It is better to say "a delicious blend of . . . " rather than "a mixture of . . . ," and so on. An evening of theater.

7. Getting Supplied

S TAPLES, fresh produce, fresh seafood, aged beef, lean lamb, meaty bacon, fresh pork sausage, pastry flour, olive oil, fresh lox, fine wines . . . where does all that stuff come from? Where, indeed. Your suppliers can be the difference between serving a high-quality meal and being just another eating place.

SUPPLIERS AND SERVICES

Here is a partial list of products and services you may require:

1. Groceries and staples
2. Meat and poultry
3. Seafood
4. Produce
5. Milk, cheese, and other dairy products
6. Bread and bakery items
7. Special ethnic food staples
8. Coffee and tea
9. Wine and beer
10. Soft drinks
11. Linen supply and laundering
12. Dishwashing machine supply and service
13. Water softener service
14. Cleaning and maintenance products
15. Gardening service
16. Printed material

Many of these items can be supplied by the same vendor. For example, fine cheeses may come from the dairy supplier, the meat and poultry supplier, or a special vendor. Your wine list may be printed by your wine distributor. There are several miscellaneous services you may require that are not listed on the preceding page. These include knife sharpening, steam cleaning, carpet cleaning, window washing, sign painting, and trash and garbage pickup. In addition, you will require a convenient source for small equipment and utensil replacement. If there is a local restaurant supply store, it will serve. Otherwise, your groceries and staples supplier will probably have a catalogue from which you can choose such items, with full return and refund privileges.

I wonder why most restaurants do not carry a wide selection of teas.

Selecting suppliers. It is likely that you will open in an area that already has at least one reasonably good restaurant. Check with the management there to find out what suppliers serve the area. But also consider the possibility that a better supplier may be willing to expand its operation to serve a new restaurant, even if it is not now delivering in the area.

If you are in a locale new to you, try to get an interview with a retired chef in the vicinity who cooked for or ran a successful restaurant. Find out what products and companies he or she held in high regard. If that is not possible, go to a nearby town or city; the chef in the best restaurant there may be willing to discuss suppliers. Call them up and talk over your plans and menu with them. The ultimate choice of who gets the bulk of your orders rests with you. You have no obligations to any of them. It is a good idea to try to have at least two suppliers for all major items in your food inventory. It keeps everyone on his toes, and often helps you to take advantage of the bargains that only the salesperson can bring to your attention each week.

Your choice of which day in the week to remain closed may hinge on which day certain important suppliers' salespeople stop at your place. You should be open for them, if possible. If you are closed that day, you may have to be at the restaurant anyway for the first few months to see the sales representative and get to know the line. Later, you can leave your orders on the back door or have the sales rep telephone you. There is never a "best" day to close—only best days to be open.

Pickup or delivery? Most suppliers of staple goods—such as grocery items, paper and cleaning products, and other packaged goods— make deliveries once a week. Fresh food suppliers will appear at least twice a week with such items as fruits and vegetables, meat, seafood, and dairy products. In the city you may be able to get daily delivery, if necessary. With once-a-week delivery, your salesperson becomes a key link in the chain that saves you when you have forgotten to order something, or they have forgotten to load it on the truck. If he cares about you, he may be able to make a special trip to get it to you, or send it up the next day with another supplier's truck coming your way.

In some remote areas, you may not find competing suppliers to serve you well. Under such circumstances you may be forced to arrange with someone in a town or city nearby that is served by a good supplier to accept deliveries that will be picked up later by you or your helper. Such arrangements are very inconvenient and expensive at best; perhaps in a mountain resort or other remote tourist area the effort is justifiable. There is simply no substitute for reliable, high-quality supplies, delivered to your door.

In general, it is worth more to you to have something delivered than to go somewhere to pick it up. You will always be offered cash-and-carry bargains in provisions at restaurant supply warehouses. But if you figure your time at $10 per hour, you usually come out the loser.

Is it really the best buy? When you use canned staples in your kitchen, take care to compare price per *net weight* pound, as well as the taste. Comparison of the case prices alone of two suppliers will not give the cost of the food accurately unless the yield per can is the same. For example, a quart can of tomatoes from one company may contain 20 percent more water than that of another company. The latter may be priced 5 percent higher, but is actually the better buy in most instances. The salesman of the higher-priced tomatoes will be happy to make an actual drain-and-weigh comparison test right in your kitchen. The old adage is generally still true: you get what you pay for. It's your job not to pay for water at the price of tomatoes.

THE SALESPERSON IS THE KEY

No supplier is perfect, nor is any salesperson. But the difference between one good supplier and another good one is the sales rep. He or she is your link to the company, whose office and warehouse may be in another city. How well you evaluate and choose your sales representatives will make the difference between good and unreliable service.

Several weeks before you open your restaurant, you will be besieged by all sorts of salespeople trying to sell you frozen food, unnecessary items of small equipment, and their special brands of goods. They will be testing you to see what you know, trying to get you started on their particular lines of products; they know that once you are hooked, you may be too busy or reluctant to change. Some may try to intimidate you into taking a minimum $500 order before they will agree to sell you the very thing that you called them about specifically. Never be intimidated by a sales rep. Here again, your ability to judge character is essential to the selection process.

A favorite trick of slightly slippery salesmen is to quote an attractive price for an expensive item, such as canned white albacore tuna; upon delivery, you discover that an unfamiliar brand has been substituted for your tried and true regular brand. Or the invoice price on delivery may be higher than the one quoted when you placed the order. Obviously, you must check each order when it arrives. Unintentional errors will occur occasionally; but the scrupulous sales rep will take pains to correct them. The case of substitute goods will be picked up with no argument and you will receive credit for it; or the invoice price will be reduced to the figure at which you ordered the goods. The latter case will be unlikely if the sales rep is deliberately "low-balling." If it happens too often, it may be time to call the district manager, or find a new supplier.

INVENTORY CONTROL

Inventory control for a small restaurant can be done quite simply if the storage shelves allow you to display your staples so that all items in stock are visually obvious. Weekly ordering thus becomes a matter of simply taking note of the stock on hand as you walk around with your order sheet. You can supplement your visual check by keeping a "needs list" for unusual or infrequently ordered items.

Many suppliers will provide you with a printed order sheet on which you can mark each week's order. If your salesperson is savvy, he may warn you of impending price increases in time for you to stock up on steadily needed items; it is usually impractical, though, to hoard too much of any one thing.

Adequate storage and refrigeration capacity will enable you to take advantage of occasional special price cuts, and should increase your profit. But the ability to hold down waste is even more important to steady profits. That will depend on your imagination in using leftovers, and on your keeping accurate records to help you plan from year to year.

Eventually someone will inadvertently fill the sugar bowls with salt. If this is the worst mixup in your restaurant, you will be fortunate. But it reminds you how important it is to taste what you serve. Moreover, it shows how imperative it is never to store any nonfood substance, such as cleaning powder, insecticide, fertilizer, or other potentially dangerous items, in a place or container where it could be mistaken for a look-alike food ingredient.

DELIVERY ROUTINE

Many sales and delivery people will walk through your back door and into your kitchen every week. Some will be regulars, who will soon learn your routine and will place the delivery where you expect to find it, or will try to avoid making a sales call right in the middle of a busy lunch. But occasionally there will be temporary replacements—a deliveryman who needs a kind word about where everything goes, or who arrives when you have no time and stands right in the middle of the kitchen. Relax. He can wait a few minutes while you finish, or you can get someone else to check the order and initial the invoice.

There is a lot to be said for making your kitchen environment one that the delivery people look forward to visiting. If the chef is glad to see the deliverer, and perhaps asks some friendly personal question, it helps make a boring day more pleasant. Occasionally a nice cool drink (no alcohol, please!) or even a short lunch can be offered. Too often the delivery person becomes the recipient of each restaurant owner's petty grievance of the day. And if these small kindnesses are not in themselves reward enough, think of this: Sales and delivery people see and talk to many, many people in their travels. Their friends and acquaintances expect them to know the good places to eat; when they speak highly of you and your restaurant, the benefit is limitless.

If you serve tourists, you and your staff may someday be unnerved by the following occurrence. One perfectly ordinary day, a big grey tour bus from Indiana will stop and a nice man will enter your establishment. You will be told tremulously that forty-four hungry people are coming in, ready or not. Their impatience to eat will be exceeded only by their inability to decide what they want. When the first is served, half of the other guests will arise to see what they got, and 50 percent of them will try to change their orders. They will drive your servers to distraction with a series of ill-timed requests, culminating with the demand for separate checks. They will all pay with $20 bills. They will each leave fifteen cents under the edge of a plate, although they loved your food and service. The above symptoms of acute constipation are a common tour-bus syndrome. The cure is to get home.

Dishwashing machine service. Of all the suppliers whose efforts do not involve food or beverage, the dishwashing supply man is the most important. When you unexpectedly run out of soap, he must respond promptly. Do not deal with anyone who will not also be able to service and repair your brand of equipment. That should mean that he carries with him a good inventory of parts, or can get them at a moment's notice. In this instance, again, the price of the soap and rinse additive may be lower elsewhere, but the availability of regular service and repairs is worth much more.

One never knows when your service people will find a chance to help you beyond the call of duty. One afternoon when it was supposed to be a normally quiet off-season day in our town, the unexpected occurred. A very large tour bus pulled up to our restaurant and disgorged its contents of hungry tourists, while a frantic tour guide asked if we could handle them. Our staff at that moment consisted of three people—a chef, a waitress, and myself—and there were ten indoor tables and eleven outdoor tables, most of which filled rapidly. I am not a chef, nor am I a really convincing waitress, but I do wield a mean wipe cloth as a busperson and I'm pretty fast with a credit-card imprinter as a cashier. My professional dishwashing experience dates from 1950; but under circumstances like this, everyone becomes the dishwasher as often as possible. It was too late to call for help, even if any had been available.

In the middle of this madhouse, when we were running out of cups, forks, iced-tea glasses, and who knows what else, who should arrive but the dishwashing machine serviceman. I spotted him on one wild pass through the kitchen and saw him smile as I shouted, "No time now!" For the next hour, on each of my trips into the kitchen with bus trays full of dirty dishes, I saw that he was still there —not working on the machine, but doing the dishes. He saved the day, the tour, and the frazzled nerves of the staff. He got more than a free lunch. He got our continued patronage when he left his company and went into the distributing and service business for himself. We could have gone with another reliable, larger firm whose product was cheaper; but one does not quickly forget service beyond what is expected.

FRESH OR FROZEN?

The pressures on restaurateurs to use other than locally grown or produced foods are very great. The vagaries of both season and suppliers tend to force you to rely on your can opener and your freezer, rather than on your local farmer, fisherman, or herdsman. The following comments are intended as counterpressure.

Seafood. Timeliness is a key to reliability, whether in a supplier or an employee. But if you specialize in serving truly fresh seafood, you will be subject to the unpredictability of the ocean, the weather, the fishing fleet, and the people who fillet fish. You will have to learn to trade off the uncertainty of delivery against the desire to serve fish that was delivered the day you serve it. (Not that it is so bad to serve fish delivered yesterday, but if you have some left over, you will gain an extra day of use if it was fresh the first day.) You will learn to recognize by touch and smell whether your fish is truly fresh upon delivery. Do not tolerate any old fish. Freshness in seafood is more important than whether it arrives exactly when promised. One advantage of having a small restaurant is that, in an emergency when an order fails to arrive, you can usually get enough of any item at a local market to get you through the day.

Some types of seafood are best delivered frozen to ensure freshness, unless you are absolutely certain of the local source of supply. These include individually quick-frozen (IQF) shrimp and prawns of all sizes, chopped clams, scallops, squid, abalone, lobster tails, king crab legs, and midwestern trout. (Note: the size of prawns, or shrimp, is designated "under x," where x equals the number of prawns it takes to make a pound; so with "under 12's," each prawn is 1⅓ ounces or more in size.) Shellfish and crustaceans spoil rapidly once they are dead. The likelihood of original freshness is greater when they are packaged frozen for shipment. Clams, oysters, and mussels are best served fresh. Frozen clams in the shell are available but not recommended.

I strongly urge you, however, to establish the reputation that when your menu says "fresh," it means the seafood served has never been frozen. It shows.

Produce. Fresh produce is essential to a menu that attempts to offer a well-balanced, nutritionally excellent meal. As the public becomes more aware of nutritional value, you will be able to establish a reputation for providing a healthful experience, as well as an elegant and joyful one. After all, isn't that what is meant by a "home-cooked" meal: one that is well-planned, nutritionally balanced, and served promptly after preparation? It is not difficult to serve fresh vegetables that have not been overcooked; and the seasonal changes in the fresh produce market build variety into your menu.

You will be able to find someone who will deliver fresh produce to you if you will be a steady customer. It is cheaper to order by the full or half crate or carton. So if you can do it profitably, you should try to plan vegetarian lunch and dinner offerings for the growing number of people who have cut down their intake of meat. Such items do not have to involve a lot of special preparation in a purposeless attempt to make them look like meatloaf or meatballs. By simply parboiling or steaming fresh vegetables and serving them with rice and perhaps cheese and a light sauce such as soy or even Hollandaise, and serving this as a main course with soup or salad, wine, and a nice dessert, you can create a special dinner. Your reputation for fresh fruit and vegetables will grow, and you will create the demand that will allow you to order in more economical bulk quantities.

Especially during the summer, you will get offers from itinerant produce vendors who specialize in tomatoes, lettuce, avocados, sweet corn, or the like. They will offer to supply you with all your produce, with big savings on their specialty. This is great while it lasts, but the reliability of a fresh food source over the entire year is worth a lot to you. Don't be too quick to switch from your old dependable supplier on price differential alone.

All produce vendors will give you the choicest goods when you first become a customer. It won't last. But if the produce delivered is partly rotten, or too old to last until the next delivery, be very firm about receiving credit. This should not happen too often. If it does, it may be time for a competitor to have a chance.

Beef. Beef is not what it was when feed corn was cheaper. To ensure proper flavor and tenderness, it will be necessary to age your beef an additional amount of time. This means that the sealed polyethylene bag in which, for example, a top sirloin is delivered *must* be intact, and must remain so during cold storage. If there is blood in the bottom of a carton of "tops," it means that one of the sealed bags is punctured, and you don't want that piece of meat unless you plan to use it immediately. Send back punctured packages if you plan to age the contents.

On occasion there may be other reasons for returning meat. Discuss in advance with your sales representative the returns policy of his company, and warn him about what you will not accept. For example, you should return items of the wrong cut, the wrong weight (significantly different from what you ordered), or the wrong portion size (chops cut at three to the pound, say, instead of four to the pound); or meat that is improperly trimmed so that there is much too much fat. If a customer reports a really tough steak (not ordered well done), and you have just cut it from a new piece, you may wish to be able to return the unused portion; this should be arranged in advance with the salesman. (Perhaps you will be grinding your own beef and can make some use of the tough meat anyway; but that is pretty expensive ground beef.)

The main point is that you must train your meat supplier to provide you with the very best quality he has unless he wants to get it back. If you are small enough to use selected meat cuts, yet big enough to be a steady customer, you should be able to insist on the best. Again, the reliability of a supplier who sends you top-quality meat is worth the few cents more per pound you may have to pay.

Truth in menu descriptions. Tell the truth on your menu. If the food is fresh, say so. If it is "fresh frozen," and the customer asks the server whether it is fresh, be certain the answer is truthful, but informative of the fact that the food is of the highest quality. Remind the customer that the meal is prepared by your chef in your own kitchen. Good frozen food is always more healthful and better tasting than food that used to be fresh.

You will find that some customers have been lied to for so long by other restaurants, especially in the big cities, that they refuse to believe you even when you tell the truth. I went fishing on my birthday one time, after our restaurant had been open for more than a year. That evening, having caught the limit of Pacific bluefish, I proudly announced to the dinner guests that the fish was absolutely fresh, since I had caught it myself. This was too much for one of our local patrons. "Don't hand me that baloney," he said emphatically. "Bring me the pork chops, and don't try to tell me you slaughtered the pig."

I learned a good lesson that day. Had I kept my mouth shut about catching the fish, he might have discovered for himself that the delicious, delicate flavor of truly fresh fish does not have to be advertised—nor can you fake it. If it is fresh and is prepared expertly, it shows.

One of the more hostile expressions in American life occurs on menus: "No Substitutions." It is the antithesis of a fine restaurant.

Precooked frozen food? If you create a small restaurant that specializes in preparing meals of high quality that compare favorably with those cooked at home, you will want to avoid the many precooked and "factory"-prepared frozen items that rarely meet the above criterion. You cannot imagine the number of food items that are on the market and touted as labor-saving, "high-profit" movers. Did you know that you can buy an extruded frozen roll of hard-cooked egg about twelve inches long? This labor-saver must be used with a special slicer, but it does produce a set of uniform slices of egg to garnish salads. And each slice looks as though it came from the widest part of the egg. Who knows what has been added to it to make it extrude uniformly, slice evenly, and keep in the freezer for up to a year?

The most flagrant example of this kind of food merchandising I have ever experienced personally occurred several years ago at a famous old seafood restaurant in Malibu, California, which had a lovely view of the Pacific Ocean surf. The place had always been known for fresh seafood, so I ordered stuffed prawns. When they arrived, I was appalled to discover they were breaded, prefrozen, and deep-fried; they lay limply on the plate, and tasted as if they were left over from the previous year. But the price of the dinner was set as if it had been prepared in the restaurant's own kitchen.

A number of old-time favorites—including scampi (which are not breaded!), chicken Kiev, stuffed boneless trout, stuffed pork chops, veal cutlets, and, believe it or not, lobster bisque—have lost their distinction under these circumstances. You may decide to revive their popularity by preparing them properly.

Restaurant owners sometimes eat at a competitor's place just to keep tabs on him. A chef I knew always served his competitor a lousy meal—not because he didn't like him, but because he wanted to keep him complacent. He reasoned that if the competitor found out how good he was, the other place would try harder and improve.

YOUR WINE STOCK

The ability to judge young, great wines and to lay them down under properly controlled conditions can be the difference between a good wine list and an outstanding one. If your restaurant becomes known for its gourmet food, a great wine list will bring the best clientele to you rather than to a competitor whose food may be equally good.

If you are interested in wines, owning a fine restaurant gives you the chance to have a lot of fun at wholesale prices. But do not place yourself at the mercy of a wine salesman who cares more about popular brands than about how the wine tastes. If you are to have a distinctive wine list, you must rely primarily on your own taste. You should supplement your judgment with that of your knowledgeable clients; ask them to suggest wines and taste them. Occasionally you may also find that a local liquor store owner or salesperson is a connoisseur of fine wine; such an adviser can be invaluable. If you are a neophyte, you should begin now by reading books, such as

Peter Quimme's lucid exposition on wine, *The Signet Book of American Wine* (Revised Edition), which is available in paperback (New American Library, 1977).

You will be limited by the amount of capital you can afford to invest in wine, by the amount of proper storage space you have, and by the price range that your patrons will accept. The wines produced in your area may also impose a limitation, but if you are really interested in wines you should make connections with suppliers of premium California wines. Or you may be able, once you are well established, to travel to California to make contact with smaller and medium-sized wineries. By the time you are ready to open, there may be successful wineries in other parts of the country, closer to you, whose products will be of use to you.

You initial wine list should be prepared with the assistance of at least two knowledgeable salespersons from suppliers who distribute fine wines in your area. They should be selected for their knowledge of wine and for their understanding of fair pricing policy. Beware of the ones who tout high profits from certain brands. Gouging the wine-drinking public is a no-no.

Your list should include a selection of three house wines (red, white, and rose), served by the glass, half-liter, and liter. The rest of the wine list should offer a number of higher-priced, better-quality red, white, rose, and dessert wines served in bottles labeled by the vintner with the name of the grape variety (or variant name) used in making the wine. The label often contains the year of harvest as well. These varietal wines are referred to in this chapter as vintage wines, to distinguish them from bulk house wines. However, this distinction is not always clear in practice. For example, a number of restaurants offer Zinfandel, a varietal wine, as one of their red house wines. Many more restaurants (and wine bottlers) offer bottles labeled with generic names that are reminiscent of areas of Europe, rather than denoting the grape variety; some even have a vintage year on the label. But the generic names for American wines bear little or no relation to the classic grape varieties used in Europe for those types of wine. These generic names include burgundy, chablis, champagne, claret, chianti, moselle, rhine, sauterne, port, sherry, and tokay, as well as other proprietary names devised by the large wineries to sound like premium varietal wines for mass market sale.

Start with a modest selection and build your wine list slowly and carefully. If you can afford it, it is nice to have a small selection of the finest wines and champagnes in the high-price category. On special occasions or by special customers such wines may be requested. They need not be included on the list, as long as someone in the dining room is well prepared to discuss wines with the customer.

The house wine. Your house wine is an important part of your offering. This is purchased in bulk quantities, such as gallons or half-gallons. Its purpose is to provide a good wine in amounts less than a bottle, or to offer the equivalent of a bottle of vintage wine at a lower price. House wines are normally served by the glass, half-liter, and liter. Some places fill an empty fifth and serve it uncorked.

If you view your house wine as merely a cheap offering, you do a disservice to the average patron who relies on your good taste. Your choice of a bulk wine should allow you to serve a wine you are proud of at a moderate price. I recommend that you choose a dry bulk wine, to satisfy the growing numbers of knowledgeable restaurant patrons who favor dry wines with food. You can accommodate the sweet wine drinkers with an inexpensive selection of fruitier wines, especially rose and light whites.

If you become known for having an excellent house wine, the volume of your sales as well as the time saved in not going through the cork-pulling ritual will make up for the perhaps smaller unit profit built into your house wine prices. You must also decide if you will carry brand-labeled wines in half-bottles, if they are available. The case price is higher per unit of wine. Therefore, the half-bottle is not as good a buy for the consumer, but it does allow the price of the evening to be held lower while including the enjoyment of a fine wine.

Some suggested wines. This book is not intended as a wine guide; but here is a list of suggested selections and starting inventory. Make your own judgments. If your wine budget is small and the availability of your selections is very certain, you can start with as little as a case of each different kind. The wineries usually offer multiple-case discounts and monthly "post-off" price reductions; these may entice you to order five or more cases at one time.

Red Varietals:	*Cases*
Dry—Pinot Noir, Zinfandel, Cabernet Sauvignon	5
Medium—Gamay, Petit Sirah, Charbono Carignane, Barbera, Baco Noir	3

Red Varietals (continued):   *Cases*

Light—Beaujolais, Gamay Beaujolais, Grenache, Ruby Cabernet	3

(Note: Vintage dry red wines should be at least 3 or 4 years old; medium red wines should be 2 or 3 years old; and light red wines 1 or 2 years old.)

Rose Wines:

Dry—Zinfandel Rose, Merlot Rose	2
Medium—Gamay Rose, Mateus, Lancers	3
Sweet—Grenache Rose, Lambrusco	1

White Varietals:

Dry—Poully Fuisse, Sauvignon Blanc (Fume Blanc), Chardonnay (Pinot Chardonnay), Dry Chenin Blanc, Pinot Blanc	5
Medium—White (Johannisberg) Riesling, Monterey Riesling, Grey Riesling, Sylvaner Riesling, Dry Semillon, White Burgundy, French Colombard, Gewurtztraminer	7
Light—Emerald Riesling, Green Hungarian, Rhine, Moselle, Liebfraumilch, Chenin Blanc, Traminer	3

(Note: Vintage white wines should be no more than 3 or 4 years old.)

House Wines:

Red—Burgundy, Zinfandel, Chianti	5 gallon cases
	7 half-gallon cases
White—Chablis, French Colombard	10 gallon cases
	12 half-gallon cases
Rose—Any not-too-sweet rose	5 gallon cases
	7 half-gallon cases

Aperitifs:

Sherries—Cream, Dry, Extra-Dry	Several bottles of each
Port—Several brands, if possible	Several bottles of each

(Note: Port should be as old as possible.)

Other—Dubonnet, Moscato Cannelli, Malvasia Bianca	One bottle

8. Staffing and Personnel Management

YOUR basic staff consists of you and your partner; your waiters, waitresses, and other optional dining room help; and your kitchen help, dishwashers, and cleanup and maintenance crew. There are some small restaurants where cleanup each night is done by a combination of the servers and cooks. This is not recommended; it is too demoralizing to have to clean thoroughly after an already hard day of serving or cooking.

From a management standpoint, there are two key positions in a restaurant. One owner should be in the kitchen, preferably as chef or assistant chef. The other must be out front in the dining room, at or near the cash drawer. There are no substitutes for these two people, except possibly a dedicated relative of one of the owners.

HIRING

You must expect all positions on your staff to have fairly high turnover. (None will have a higher turnover than dishwashing.) If you are properly prepared, however, you should have less trouble finding replacements than the larger, less personal restaurants. Yours should be one of the best places in town to work. A small restaurant's staff is like a family. If it is a happy and prosperous one, many will wish to be adopted into it.

All hiring must be the result of a two-step process. First, each prospective employee must fill out a short application. Then, each applicant must have a personal interview. The first step provides you with a record you can keep in a file for future reference; it becomes a part of your minimal personnel records. The interview gives you the most direct evidence for deciding whether the person will fit into your "family."

Make a big fuss over staff members on their birthdays.

Employment application form. You really need very little information about each prospect that is bona fide occupational qualification data. Strictly speaking, the name, address, telephone number, date of application, and previous experience, with references to former supervisors, are all you can expect to get that is of real value. You will not need to know marital status or Social Security number until after you hire, when you must figure out the withholding allowances for tax purposes. Detailed personal health information is not often requested on such applications. And most states no longer require restaurant workers to have a current Food Handler's Certificate, which was a way to screen all such employees for tuberculosis and other communicable diseases.

You will be very interested in whether your prospect lives close enough to the restaurant to be able to get to work easily. You will also want to be able to reach him or her by telephone at any time; therefore, at least a message phone is essential. Other vital data might include age (if alcoholic beverage service is involved), whether the applicant has adequate personal transportation, what hours of employment he is willing to accept, what positions in the restaurant he is willing to accept, whether or not he smokes tobacco, and whether he speaks any foreign languages. Each of these items may be relevant to your operation or personal preference for employees.

Previous employment. This information is of greatest use to you in deciding whether your prospect should be hired as a trainee or an old hand. You may wish to avoid the problems of training a server from scratch, although there are managers who want only those workers who have not yet established any bad habits. Grace and

Front

Mr. ☐			
Ms. ☐ _____		Date _____	
		Phone _____	
Address			
POSITION DESIRED: _____		Age _____	

PREVIOUSLY EMPLOYED BY:	How long?	Reason for Leaving
1.		
2.		
3.		
4.		

DUTIES	Full or part time	SUPERVISOR'S NAME
1.		
2.		
3.		
4.		

Back

REMARKS:

PERSONAL REFERENCES:

Name & Address	Phone	Relationship
1.		
2.		
3.		

Applicant Signature

Sample Employment Application Card

personality are more important than years of experience, but a little restaurant experience is better than none at all. You should qualify the experience listed on the application by asking detailed questions about the kind of place the applicant worked at, and the nature of the duties he or she performed there. The reason why employment was terminated at each place is a useful bit of information, especially if it is a local reference and can be followed up. If you are already familiar with the other restaurant, you will be better able to evaluate the reasons your prospect gives for having left.

Experience and traits to look for. What experience counts? Someone who has worked in a variety of restaurant positions, including dishwasher, will have a better understanding of any job you have available. You may find out more about an experienced waitress by the questions she asks you, rather than the other way around. Often, an applicant will have already asked a lot of questions of one of your employees.

Basically, you are interested in whether the applicant has worked in a restaurant with a similar atmosphere to yours, and whether the responsibilities assigned were relevant to your operation. If you are looking for a lunchtime kitchen assistant to make salads and sandwiches and who also can work during the day shift to prepare for the dinner service, it would be best to find someone who had done those tasks elsewhere. However, someone with table service experience in a place that served sandwiches and salads would be far better qualified than another applicant with no restaurant experience at all.

Do not hire anyone who will make somebody lose his appetite.

Some of the characteristics to look for in restaurant workers are honesty, quickness, a pleasant voice, and a look of cleanliness. It is difficult to describe the characteristics of those people whom you will not want to hire to serve your customers. But there are a few that are so obvious that I list them only as an exercise. The following list of B.F.O.D.'s (bona fide occupational disqualifications) for any restaurant worker is strictly unofficial:

1. Obesity
2. Diseased teeth
3. Skin eruptions or disease
4. Unpleasant voice

5. Hostile attitude	8. Slovenly grooming
6. Alcoholism	9. Generally poor health
7. Chronic body odor	10. Stubbornness

Keeping a reference file of applicants. The application card should have a space on the back in which you can note answers to your questions as well as other observations you make during the interview. By using a three-by-five or four-by-six index card, you will make it easier to keep a file of those applicants who can be called on short notice. The file should be culled every six months or so to weed out old applications.

You may believe that you have no openings at the moment a good prospect comes in to apply for a job, but that situation can change overnight. It is only fair to state the facts to an applicant, but it is to your advantage to have the application on file for later reference. If your reputation as a fair and honest employer accompanies your excellent name for food, you will undoubtedly be visited by many qualified people. Be sure to determine whether the applicant is currently employed at another local place. If so, ask how much notice is expected before the new job could be started. That will give you a clue as to how much concern the person has for the problems of running a restaurant.

The probationary period. Every new hire should be on a temporary basis until initial impressions are confirmed. The probationary period may be as short as a week or as long as a month, but it should be made formal. Perhaps the starting pay can allow for a small raise after a month's probation. With servers, look during the probationary period for signs that spell later trouble. Does the new server continue to forget simple little instructions? Are there frequent mistakes in addition, multiplication, tax computation? Are checks completed with all food and beverages accounted for? Any unpleasant personality traits will show up at your tables under stressful conditions. Ask your regular customers for their candid opinions of the new person.

SELECTING SERVERS

When screening applicants, look carefully at the handwriting or printing on the application. If the chef would not be able to read it easily, perhaps you should disqualify the applicant. I recommend that both the chef and the dining room supervisor take part in interviewing and evaluating server applicants.

You may be located in an area where there is a good selection of both male and female serving people. I see no reason why some restaurants restrict the use of waiters to evenings and waitresses to lunch and breakfast. It is the service that counts. The image is important, too, but it can be equally fine for male and female servers who have been properly selected and trained. Your personal preference, restaurant style, and decor will help determine whether to use a costume, distinctive uniform, or other identification for your servers. It is not legal to hire only male or only female servers.

It may be permissible for you to discriminate on the basis of size, hair style or length, or other personal features if you can establish it as a bona fide occupational qualification for your restaurant. For example: if, for your Victorian-style dining room, you decide to dress your staff all in top hat and tails, striped pants and spats, and short hair parted down the middle, a female applicant who is willing to comply with those rules has a right to be considered and hired, if she is otherwise as qualified as anyone else you hire. If you tried to limit hiring to blondes, you would have to show why a server in a blonde wig was not qualified, if it came to an actual case. I strongly advise you to consider and hire both males and females on the basis of gracefulness, personality, and a friendly face.

A klutz should not work in a restaurant.

TRAINING

I firmly believe that at some time in each person's restaurant career he should wash dishes as a full-time job—preferably as his first experience in a restaurant. It is a good question to ask prospective servers: "Have you ever been a dishwasher?"

Training your staff to do things the way you want them done is one point on which you will have to be firm. There may very likely be someone in your employ who has more restaurant experience than you do. That is very good, if he has learned that each place does things differently. His suggestions should be welcome, and often may be useful to you. But your style is your style. Some issues will simply relate to the policies that you wish reflected to the customer.

Other issues may directly affect profits, such as the size of a portion. If the cheesecake is to be cut into twenty-four pieces, that means that your waitress cannot decide to cut it into twenty pieces because she likes to serve bigger pieces.

The chef is the key to training servers on attitude. A sensitive chef will suppress outbursts of temper at the peak of the dinner hour by limiting herself to a grouch or two. The pressure of daily performances will affect even the best of restaurant staffs. A good crew always returns to pleasant relationships after the rush is over.

If you want to see something really funny, watch the expression on the face of the chef when a waitress is acting up. As soon as the order has been picked up and the waitress has turned and started out to the dining room, the chef will exhibit some of the most amazing grimaces imaginable. But when the chef is having a snit, watch your best waitress as she comes into view of the diners. If she is really good, no matter how bad she feels or how difficult a time she has had in the kitchen, the customer will see only the most benign look of equanimity. Maybe there is a hidden clue. Hire unemployed mimes, and your success is assured.

The bearer of compliments to the chef should deliver them as soon as possible, especially when something else has gone wrong. But a minor complaint ought to be handled without involving the chef, if possible. At least it should be reported at a time when it won't make the kitchen mood worse.

Staff meetings. As in any business, it is essential to the success of your operation to hold periodic staff meetings. Arrange them at the most convenient time for the most people, even if some have to make a special trip. The meeting will provide an opportunity for the staff to suggest ways to improve the operation, as well as for you to give everyone the chance to react as a group to your ideas and rules. Keep staff meetings short and hold them infrequently.

Feeding the staff. Your rules for staff feeding will require some strict understanding. As a general rule you should insist that your employees arrive at work ready to work, not to eat. You must specify which food items may not be served to the staff unless offered by the chef or owner. Staff people should eat at the staff table at the appointed time. If they join friends at a customer table, they should first take off aprons or other "on duty" items of clothing; otherwise the public will assume they are still on duty and resent their inattention.

If you serve alcoholic beverages, it is imperative that you control their consumption by the staff. That means no one drinks on the job, and no one gets a free beer unless one of the owners offers or approves it. (There will be times when a glass of champagne makes the difference between making it through the shift with a smile and making an enemy of a good customer.)

You are feeding your staff for your own benefit, not theirs. It keeps them conveniently on the premises, it provides quick energy when they need it, and it keeps the "family" happy. If your chef is wise, the staff meals will be selected and timed to provide an additional reward for good effort. Sometimes the real reason why a dishwasher or cleanup man will continue to work for you is that he can eat better at your place than at any other.

> *If business is slow and you want someone to walk into your restaurant, just sit down to eat. Within five minutes, someone will interrupt you.*

There is a famous restaurant in Morro Bay, California whose owner is one of the most gracious hosts in the business. He is a connoisseur of fine wine, and his wine list reflects it. After closing, when he and his staff sit down for dinner, he pops a cork to introduce the serving people to his latest wine acquisition, or to refresh their taste of an old standby. As a result, his servers are able to recommend wines intelligently to their dinner guests. And their own dinner is a time they look forward to at the end of a hard evening's work.

Dishwasher blues. "Where am I going to find another dishwasher at this late hour? We're going to have a horribly busy night, too!" Sometime in your restaurant career you will find yourself speaking or hearing these words. It might seem that the job of washing dishes is not an important one. But there is really no job in a restaurant that is less important than another, excepting chef.

Washing dishes is not an easy job, yet it is considered in many restaurants to be a task fit only for semi-competents who can't do anything else. Managers with that attitude have no one to blame but themselves if the job is done without grace and care for the dinnerware. Dishwashers usually deserve more pay than they receive. One way of making up for that is to provide better fringe benefits, such as an extra meal or extra time off. In the long run, no dishwasher, whether good or bad, will stay long at the job. If a dishwasher is really clumsy or slow, he must be replaced as soon as possible. If one is quick and careful, give her a raise, be nice, and maybe she'll stay past Labor Day. We have had both male and female dishwashers. It is too hard a job for anyone who is not long on stamina. A lot depends on whether the dishwashing area is kept cool and whether the kitchen staff is able to interact well with the dishwasher. The job is made easier by busing tables so that the bus trays may be emptied efficiently in groups of utensils, rather than making the dishwasher pick out napkins and silverware from between plates.

SCHEDULING PART-TIME WORKERS

It is quite likely that your staff will include very few full-time people other than you and your partner. The weekly work schedule is an important factor in keeping your part-time workers on their toes. The server's schedule can be a crucial determinant of tip earnings and of status. (Yes, Virginia, there is a pecking order in every restaurant.) You will have to use the weekly schedule as a tool to try to even up everyone's chances of earning good tips.

Unless you serve only dinner, you should schedule your most experienced servers for the dinner period. The busiest nights should be rotated among them all. Normally, tips are better at dinner and smart serving people will ask for a night schedule. But if you have a good, reliable staff established for dinner, and you have an opening for a daytime server, do not make the mistake of promising the applicant that he or she will be able to move to dinner work. Any really excellent daytime server who would enhance the dinner staff can always be offered the promotion later.

If your business is seasonal, or at least varies from day to day, you will soon learn the pattern. You must know the times that are likely to be busy ones and arrange your staff schedule accordingly. Be certain to keep daily records of the number of people served at each meal. These records are crucial to the next year's planning. Make notes on holidays or special events in your town that bring more business your way. Any extrapolation from the past is imperfect, however. There will be days when you have too many people working to handle a scant business. If you can, send someone home early. Or perhaps you can arrange for someone close by to be on call.

Do not allow substitutions in the work schedule without your prior approval. When you schedule a waitress for a busy weekend and you know that she would rather spend it with her boyfriend, be prepared to go to the limit on the issue. If someone else is able to fill in for her, and it is convenient for you, fine. But double shifts make for exhausted servers; and you must have final control.

It boils down to one hard fact: when you work in the restaurant business, you do not usually get the same holidays that normal people take. If you need the job, you work when you are scheduled; and you do not call in sick unless you are. If someone cannot accept the schedule, he cannot work for you. (Obviously, there are reasonable exceptions and alternatives. But you can go crazy trying to please everyone.)

At our place, if anyone was found to be smoking dope on the job, he no longer had a job, unless he could prove he had glaucoma, a serious eye ailment relieved by marijuana. A few of our staff thought they were catching glaucoma for a while, but it is not a communicable disease.

QUIT OR DISMISSED?

The work schedule may also be used to try to get a slipping performer to quit so that you don't have to dismiss him or her. If business is slowing down, the poorest performer is usually given the fewest hours to work. If the person cannot afford to work so few hours, he will sometimes look for another job. If he complains, that may be a good time to suggest that he try to find a better-paying job.

This method is not entirely satisfactory, from a number of viewpoints. It may just make the problem worse for a while until you take the bull by the horns and fire the guy. In the long run, it pays to do it honestly. If the employee no longer has the desire or has not developed the skill to do the job the way you and your customers want it done, tell him to find another job. If possible, give notice or pay in lieu of notice. Do it without recrimination or arguments to try to justify the unpleasantness. Even though it is not easy for a nice, creative person like you to fire someone, you are most likely doing him a favor. If you cannot stand to have the person working for you, it will eventually affect him badly, or it might contribute to your business failure. So do a favor for the two of you and move the unsatisfactory employee out.

SUMMER RESORT LABOR

If you happen to be located in a summer resort area, Labor Day weekend is an important milestone in your business cycle. It signals the end of the busy season. It can also be the point at which you are ready to collapse because two weeks earlier half your summer crew decided to leave for their own vacations.

It works like this. Along about May, you will be accosted at all hours by eager young people who want summer jobs. When asked, they will all promise to start work immediately after school is out and stay on until after Labor Day weekend. Do not believe it. If these folks have been in school all year until early June, work hard all summer, and have not had any vacation, by mid-August they will begin to get very dissatisfied with life. Some will leave it at that. Others will quit and take a vacation, now that they have some money saved up.

There are two ways to handle the problem. One is to try to hold off starting them at work until just before July Fourth, and to tell them to take two weeks of vacation right after school lets out, even if they have to borrow the money for it. The other method is to hire them with the strict understanding that their hourly wage will depend on whether they stay through Labor Day weekend. That is, if they expect to be paid $5 per hour, they will receive $4 of it on each payday, with the remaining dollar per hour payable at the end of the summer. That way, if they quit early, you will have some money with which to hire someone else in a hurry or to pay your loyal crew an extra bonus for working harder. This method may not be possible if you are paying minimum wages. Check with your state labor department first.

9. Cleanup and Maintenance

S O YOU hate housework and you think you will open your own restaurant? There is no end—and there are no shortcuts—to the cleaning and maintenance of an operating restaurant. The only thing that really cuts grease is elbow grease. If you are acquainted with a compulsive cleaner, hire him or her and pay a little bit more than the going rate.

DAILY CLEANUP AFTER CLOSING

Each day the kitchen should be cleaned completely following the last meal served for the day. (This simple rule must be understood at the front desk when late arrivals plead to be allowed to eat after you have closed.) Once the kitchen is closed, all food is immediately put away and cleanup begins. If it is not done until the next morning, you allow the vermin army to establish a beachhead from which further assaults will be repulsed only with great difficulty.

If the chef is the one who must clean up each night, and does not have competent help, either the chef or the restaurant will not last more than a few years. A good chef will clean up in small ways all day, however; and conscientious food preparation assistants will continually wipe and gather up garbage around the work area. Do not allow the development of an attitude that "the cleanup crew will get it."

Traditionally, cleanup begins with the cleaning of the griddle by rubbing it with a block of volcanic pumice and cooking oil. The release of the natural sulfur in the griddle block is a subtle signal that the day is coming to a sometimes exhausted close. A small putty knife completes the job of scraping the pumiced oil from the corners of the griddle. There is nothing like a shiny griddle to make the chef feel good in the morning.

Kitchen surface cleaning is accomplished with the aid of a plastic spray bottle filled with a mixture of water and vinegar. It is applied liberally and wiped with a clean towel. There are commercial solvents of all sorts which maintenance supply salesmen will try to sell you, but it is hard to beat the cost-effectiveness of vinegar water. Beware the stainless-steel polish that is oil-based. If it smells like something you would not want to have your food taste of, forget it. It was made for looks, not sanitation.

Constant wiping, scrubbing, and shining of kitchen surfaces—vertical, horizontal, and otherwise—is the only sure way to keep them clean. The main horizontal surface in the kitchen is the floor—and it is thus the recipient of everything that doesn't get caught by the ceiling, walls, shelves, and equipment. It's just like at home, only much worse. The floor supplies the dirt to be tracked everywhere else in the restaurant. Sometimes the maitre d' will wonder whence came a trail of cantaloupe seeds through the dining room. A visit to the disaster scene in the dishroom would have answered the question. Clumsy John is working this shift and he can't seem to find the center of the garbage pail—only the edge.

The floor should be swept several times per day just to keep it from getting too grungy before the night cleanup crew gets to it. The kind of floor surface you must have to meet the health code was discussed in Chapter 4. Almost any surface used to create a hard nonskid floor surface requires periodic renewal to keep it functional. Be certain that your cleaning agent, grease cutter, or other substances used daily do not cause pitting or breakdown of the kitchen floor surface. The old standby for restaurants used to be ceramic tile. Now even concrete floors (which are so devastating to your legs and feet) can be surfaced with a type of plastic-based deck paint developed for boats. It allows for excellent cleaning results without being too slippery, and it can be renewed quickly.

Any type of food slicer or processor, whether it is a big attachment to a mixer or a simple vegetable slicer, must be completely taken apart and cleaned after every day that it is used. Meat grinders and electric slicers such as those used in a delicatessen have crannies that you can't begin to imagine unless you have personally taken one apart to clean it of food particles. I recommend you do so several times so you can check on your cleanup crew.

PERIODIC CLEANING

The restaurant health code usually requires that certain kinds of maintenance be performed on a regular basis. The same logic applies to the cleaning chores that are under your direct control. You should impose a strict periodic cleaning schedule on every piece

CLEANING SCHEDULE

DAILY	WEEKLY	PERIODICALLY
Griddle & range	Grease filters	Freezers
Steam table	Refrigerators	Dishwashing machine nozzles & reservoir
Sinks, drainboards, & backsplash	Grease trap	
	Windows	
Microwave oven	Remove carpet spots	Storeroom
Dishwashing machine & drainboard	Wash all dispensers for salt, pepper, sugar, honey, syrup	Hidden corners in kitchen and behind equipment
Kitchen floor		
Appliances & equipment surfaces	Clean all shelving	Vacuum dust on vanes of refrigeration compressor units
Rest room sinks, toilet, mirror, & floor	Clean all crevices in shake mixer, drink dispenser, milk dispenser, toaster, slicer, coffee maker, hot-fudge machine, syrup dispenser, etc.	
		Wipe down walls
Dining room carpet & floor		Steam-clean accumulated grease in ducts, etc.
Tables & chairs		
Coffee machine	Polish woodwork	Drain lines in sinks

TABLE 3. *Cleaning Schedule for a Small Restaurant*

of equipment used in the kitchen. (See Table 3.) The most important of these are the grease filters in the exhaust hood and the grease interceptor (or trap) in the sewer line. The drain lines from sinks require attention to abate grease buildup, especially if they run horizontally for more than a few feet before dropping into the main line.

Garbage disposers in sinks that grind up food wastes create a special problem for drain lines. You are much better off saving all your edible garbage for someone who raises pigs. Get in touch with your local 4-H club to find out about nearby pig farmers. If you are in a city where no one will contract for daily pickup of your edible garbage, or in a municipality that prohibits the use of grinders with private sewage disposal systems, you must be prepared to hold your garbage in tightly closed containers, to prevent animals or vermin from getting at it, until the garbage service picks it up.

Periodic cleaning and maintenance are also essential for automatic dishwashers, the hot-water booster and heater, and the ductwork for the kitchen exhaust system. The blower fan is another item that can suffer grease buildup. The rooftop grease pan that is sometimes installed below the exhaust blower air outlet must be cleaned and checked. Many a restaurant fire has occurred because the ductwork was ignored for too long, even though the kitchen was kept clean. For ease of maintenance, the ducts should be exposed, if possible.

If your restaurant is so small that you have decided against installing an automatic dishwasher, you will be using a sink with a disinfectant rinse to wash your kitchen equipment. But this does not remove grease film as well as does the 180° F rinse in an automatic washer. Therefore, I recommend that you try to arrange for a service that operates portable steam-cleaning equipment. Have them come around several times a year to steam clean your exhaust grease filters and other kitchen equipment thoroughly. It will probably not cost too much if they are not too far away or can come regularly for several customers. You may have to contract for a year's service.

Cleaning out the grease trap. The location of the grease trap can present an odor and temperature problem, as discussed in Chapter 4. Though it must be cleaned more often, the great advantage of a small grease trap, as opposed to a large one, is that the cleaning job is accomplished in a relatively short time. You must determine the schedule for cleaning by your observation of the need, the type of menu you have, the habits of the preparation crew in draining grease in the sink, and how much business you have. If possible, it is best not to dispose of grease in the sewer line at all, but to pour it into a container, seal it tightly, and put it out with the trash. Wipe out as much grease as possible with paper towels.

The best way to clean a grease trap is with a clothespin and a modified metal ladle-like utensil originally designed for lifting large pieces out of a deep pot. The ladle has a shallow bowl, with holes to allow the liquid to drain. But this type of ladle always has a circular bowl, and your grease trap has square corners. So you must make the utensil workable by bending up two edges of the ladle to create a corner with two adjacent lips at right angles that will fit nicely up against the sides of the trap. Using this simple device, you can ladle up the semisolid grease at the top of the trap without taking the dirty water beneath it. When you open the trap and find a lot of grease and not much water, that means you are not cleaning the trap frequently enough. The clothespin is for your nose. If you insist on watching your cleanup man do it, you will need two clothespins.

Treat the man who repairs your refrigeration with sweet gentleness.

SIDEWORK

"Sidework" is an activity that any experienced server performs when not otherwise busy. It refers to the 101 items around a restaurant that need to be wiped, cleaned, and polished. It is not busywork. The accumulations of dust, greasy film, and general spills and residues in the most unlikely places must be constantly sought out and removed. Sidework fills the interstices of a shift with activity that justifies having two servers working even though one and one-half servers could easily handle the customers.

Your servers and dishwashers are your first line of defense against the relentless advance of grease buildup. It will happen anyway, despite your best efforts. This is why most health codes require periodic repainting of restaurant kitchens, and also why all kitchen surfaces including the ceiling must have a hard, smooth finish. (Ever try to wipe down a tongue-in-groove pine ceiling?) Corners can collect enough food for an army of roaches, and you are not the commander-in-chief of that army. Just let one word get around that someone found a cockroach in one of your dinners and you will have a more difficult time eradicating that story than you will getting rid of the pests.

Dust is a kitchen phenomenon that does its work slowly but effectively. You must vacuum it away from the grid on the condenser of each piece of refrigeration. These parts are usually hidden from view behind a panel so that the dust is not blown on the food. But you had better find them. The shelving in the kitchen may be all stainless steel, if you had a huge budget. But dust can be wiped away just as well from plain pine boards that have been properly treated with a hard finish such as varnish or polyurethane plastic.

THE DINING ROOM FLOOR

Caring for your floors other than the one in the kitchen may require some special equipment. If you have carpeting in the dining room, it should have a short, hard nap, and should be vacuumed daily with an upright commercial machine such as a Kirby. All sorts of stuff will be ground into your carpet, so it is best to choose a color and design that will blend in well with the spots of salad dressing, raisins, sour cream, strawberry preserves, hot fudge sauce, coffee, steak fat, soy sauce, and cooked carrots. The table area where you usually place the high chair for infants will be a special carpet maintenance target. The only way to avoid having to replace the carpet too often is to use a can of spot lifter on each evening's or each week's spills. (It is good to have a couple of cans of spot remover around anyway, to take care of occasional spills on a customer's clothing. It works quite well on most fabrics.)

If your floor is not carpeted, you will probably need to use a mop and buffer; or perhaps you will have a kind of surface that does not require buffing. Uncarpeted flooring can be quite noisy unless it is on a cement slab. Your decor may not call for carpeting, but it is the floor covering that looks best while it lasts, and it is almost as easy to maintain as a washable floor. It hides wear better than most other surfaces.

REST ROOM MAINTENANCE

Your objective is to keep the rest room from being a problem to your customers. They should be even more pleased with your service after a visit to the rest room than before. A few simple rules will help achieve that goal.

The rest rooms should be stocked with a hand soap that is germicidal, not just sweet-smelling. Get the concentrated liquid kind used in hospitals, and dilute it with water. I prefer liquid soap dispensers over powdered or bar soap. They are less of a mess and easier to keep clean, and there is less waste. Folded paper hand towels in dispensers result in a basketful at the end of the day. But they are less unsightly than the continuous-roll cotton toweling that hangs, covered with dirty hand prints, like a towel at a boys' camp. You may have the money to invest in one of those fancy hot-air blowers with the funny adjustable nozzle you can turn up to dry your face. Does anyone ever really dry his face with one of those things?

Keep your bathroom supply dispensers full and in good operating order. It is unlikely in a small restaurant that any dispenser of paper or soap will run out during any single mealtime. Therefore, you will avoid trouble if you check and replenish supplies before each meal service. A patron who is forced to use a paper towel instead of toilet paper will very likely cause an overflow. In such cases it is nice to have more than one rest room available so that the one with the problem can be temporarily closed until the floor is mopped.

The other potential problems with rest rooms revolve around illness and discomfort. If a patron is drunk, sick, or unhappy with someone at the table, he or she frequently ends up in the rest room. And you may be left with a mess to clean up. It helps to have a cabinet or closet designed right into the rest room for storing the cleaning supplies that will make the job easier and quicker. I believe that the more your rest room design and decor remind the patron of home, rather than an institution, the less likely he is to make a mess of it. Keep it simple and familiar.

10. Advertising and Public Relations

THERE is only one sure method of advertising for the small restaurant. When you serve an outstanding meal to a delighted customer, he becomes an effective and consistent source of advertising. As such a person leaves your front door, do not hesitate to encourage his assistance. As an old restaurant adage has it, "If you liked it, please tell your friends. If you didn't, please tell us."

GETTING YOUR NAME KNOWN

Your building is an advertisement. The tasteful use of lettering and color, whether in the form of brilliant flowers, a mural, a mosaic, or any other attractive artwork outdoors, should send a message from you to anyone who goes by.

It is worth directing some effort toward establishing good word-of-mouth recommendations in your community, whether it is a small town or a neighborhood of a big city. It is not complicated. After you have been open for a few weeks and your routine has gelled, invite some local businesspeople to enjoy a complimentary meal at your place. If possible, do it for an organized group, such as the local motel association; otherwise, invite managers individually. The targets of these efforts should be those people most likely to be asked where in town there is a good place to eat. They include managers of motels, gas stations, tourist-oriented businesses, executive secretaries in industry, local politicians, and people who man chamber of commerce information desks. Remember, too, the local office of the automobile association. Pour your house wine generously, and serve a lovely meal. Your investment will come back to you tenfold.

Public relations boils down to a few simple precepts. Be honest in your advertising, in your dealings with customers and creditors, and with your employees. When a mistake is made, give the other person the benefit of the doubt by assuming at the outset that there was a failure to understand. Apologize first for your mistakes, then compensate. Answer all your mail promptly and with style. Assist those in trouble if they come to you, even if it is not on the menu. Send some hot soup in a thermos to the sick child of a traveler at the motel. Give the runaway an hour or two of work picking up the trash in your parking lot and sweeping the sidewalk, and pay with a good meal and a few bucks. Public relations is simply having empathy and acting on it in a way that serves others. It won't work if you view it as a chore or quid pro quo.

I despair for the traveling public each time I am told, "We have been on the road for three weeks now, and this is the first *meal we have had that makes us feel as good as we do at home. It was delicious."*

Build up interest beforehand. Plan your advertising campaign well in advance of your opening, so that it can be carried out in a reasonable and economical way. The first ads might even appear as "ticklers" during the last few weeks before you open. For several weeks before the opening of the Grey Fox Inn, the following ads appeared in our local newspaper with our fox logo:

First week: a tiny display ad saying just, "The Fox."
Second week: a small ad saying, "The Fox is coming."
Third week: a larger ad saying, "The Fox is coming soon!"
Fourth week: a large ad saying, "The Fox is here!"
The last one contained a full description of the restaurant location, hours, and type of meals available.

Display advertising. When you advertise in a newspaper or magazine, design your display ad thoughtfully. Use an easily recognizable visual feature such as a logo or special lettering for your name, and aim for readability with a clear, appropriate typeface, a few lines in a bolder type, and plenty of white space. It is not difficult to learn what the newspaper people have to do to prepare your ad for

THE
BOGUS
RESTAURANT
Seafoods and fancy country fare

Brunch every Sunday 11 to 3, $8 per person

Hours: Monday–Thursday 11:30 a.m. to 9 p.m.
Friday–Saturday 11:30 a.m. to 10 p.m., Sunday 11 a.m. to 9 p.m.

Uptown Center, Someplace, Pennsyltucky ● 555-4444

A good display advertisement is both elegant and specific.

print. If you are going to advertise regularly, but will change part of the text periodically, you should understand what is easy to change and what cannot be changed readily just before the deadline. In general, plan to use the same framework and art in your ad each time it appears, changing only the typeset portion within. If you have a logo or picture you will often want included, try to obtain at least a dozen photostats of them in different sizes so that you can use them for other ads in other publications later.

A one-column-inch ad is one column wide by one inch high. A four-column-inch ad may be one column wide by four inches high, or four columns wide by one inch high, or two columns wide by two inches high.

Always try to arrange to check a proof of your ad, or at least check the wording by telephone after the ad is laid out. Mistakes will be made, in any case, despite everyone's wish to avoid them. If you cannot check the copy beforehand, be sure to do so as soon as the publication hits the street. If there is an error, you can at least limit it to that one issue.

Some newspapers have a restaurant page where most such ads are concentrated. Whether or not to use it is a question for empirical results to answer. Try it both ways to see if one spot is more effective than the other. Some papers will ask you to sign up for three months of advertising on their "business directory" page, and will promise to run a feature story about your restaurant on that page once during that period. This whole idea, which presents advertising thinly disguised as news, is not high on the list of good newspaper practices. But so many papers, especially weeklies, do it that you might as well take advantage of it. If you can write well, perhaps you will even be allowed to write the feature article yourself.

News items and reviews. A real news item about your place, in any case, is always better than an advertisement. If there is a restaurant guide or critical review section in your town or city newspaper, get in touch with the editor of that feature. Write up a succinct and interesting news release—perhaps including a recipe for one of your chef's specialties—and set up an arresting black-and-white photograph to go with it. In a big city, the restaurant critic will be thoughtful enough to wait until you have settled in a bit before visiting, but your news release might fill an empty space on the food page. If you are in a small town, the weekly paper may run one story about your opening just out of courtesy. And you can usually get your press release into one of the free "advertiser" papers that are delivered to every doorstep in many neighborhoods.

If you are located in a small town, the following comments are directed specifically to you in relation to your small-town newspaper. The economy of a small community is a wondrous and fragile thing; and one of the principal links that holds the whole entity together is the community newspaper. Steady advertising revenue is absolutely essential to the survival of any paper, especially one in a small town. Decide realistically what you can afford, but advertise regularly. And pay your bill each time it is presented. Especially in a restaurant, you will get business in return for such good habits.

The interdependence of people in a small community is what caused this country to evolve its abiding character. There is a rebirth of recognition of this going on all over the nation as a counterforce to the impersonal relationships and violence of the megalopolis. It is a reaction, as well, against the corporate balance-sheet bottom-line mentality that spawned, for example, the epidemic of franchised "fast food" farces that claim to be restaurants. The small restaurant and such other individual enterprises as local craftsmen, merchants, and newspapers are a vital part of the counterforce. If you open your restaurant as a way of living in a small town, your obligation to the small-town newspaper is clear. It doesn't matter whether or not you agree with the publisher's politics; the children of your waitresses and the children of his advertising representative deserve to live in a vital small town with a good restaurant and a good newspaper.

REACHING TOURISTS

When you consider advertising in a magazine-type publication oriented toward visitors to your town, city, or region, you must be very certain of the effectiveness of the format and the distribution method. For example, a brochure placed directly in each motel room, passed out to each automobile rental customer, or mailed directly to convention registrants, is more likely to attract visitors than the same item sitting on a counter or rack in the lobby. The total number of such brochures printed is less meaningful than the number actually placed in the hands of prospective customers. Also, take a look at other publications the same outfit has produced before you take an ad. Sometimes their quality is so poor that your being included can do more harm than good.

The cost of this kind of advertising can be quite high. Do your best to see that your ad has high recognition value and is placed in an appropriate spot in the publication. As a general rule, an ad should return at least 110 percent of its cost in profit dollars to make it worthwhile.

The telephone book. The telephone book is a form of advertising that requires advance planning. Find out the deadline for listings in both the white and yellow pages, relative to your opening. You cannot have a white-pages listing unless you have a telephone. If the deadline is in October, but you will not open until January, it might pay to install the restaurant phone in your home or an office near your location, just to get the listing. When calls come in, you can explain that you plan to open in January, and request that the caller try again then. When you finally do open, the telephone can be transferred to the restaurant.

You can use the same technique with the yellow pages. If you can afford a display ad, use the space to describe your restaurant and advise the reader to call for directions. The monthly charge may be worth it to you to be in the book for the better part of the year that you intend to open. After your first year, you can decide if you really need a display ad, or if the alphabetical listing under Restaurants, with a few extra lines of description, will suffice. The yellow pages may have another restaurant list broken down by nationality of cuisine. Go for it, if it applies to your place.

Your menu is an ad. Place copies of your menu at strategic locations such as motel desks, car rental agencies at the airport, and other places that guide the traveler. Don't overlook bulletin boards in such places as laundromats, supermarkets, and miniature golf courses. And don't hesitate to give a menu to anyone who asks for one; charge a nominal fee if necessary.

Billboards. I can think of no instance except for major emergencies in which the use of billboards is better than a large display ad in a widely read publication, or a spot on television, or in any medium that does not spoil the look of the countryside and the architecture of our cities. Posting bills on smaller kiosks at appropriate visitor centers would serve the people who never look at other media, and would not contribute ugliness on such a grand scale.

Having said all this, if outdoor advertising space is available in your area at a reasonable cost, you should consider its use at least until you are better known and established. But get the best sign painter you can find to design your ad for you. Perhaps you can cooperate with other businesses in your immediate area to place a multiple-services sign at an opportune location.

When you travel, do not rely on billboard signs. The best way to discover an excellent small restaurant is to visit a local business establishment and ask the owner or salesperson where in town he goes to eat.

RADIO

Radio advertising can be quite effective if the announcer has first-hand knowledge of your restaurant. When an announcer talks about the luscious scampi he had the other night at your place, he can actually make people's mouths water. The personal rapport attained on both FM and AM radio can have a striking effect, if done well. But you must arrange to have the disc jockey or station manager eat at your restaurant before he or she performs the advertising spots.

Most radio spot commercials are set for fifteen, thirty, or sixty seconds, and broadcast during a particular time slot on predetermined days. If you contract for longer periods you may get a price break or better choice of time. To prepare a properly focused radio campaign you must become familiar with local programming formats and audiences. Ask the station representative for verified listener profiles when preparing to select your station or stations. You can have several ad scripts prepared and used in rotation or to fit the day of the week and time of day. Be certain to listen to your ad or have the final scripts sent to you before you approve the broadcast.

The FM stations that pipe music into offices and department stores may be of help to you in drawing local employees. They are always looking for a nice place to go, to escape from that piped-in music. The type of music played on the station pretty well determines the market you will appeal to. If you wish to attract classical music lovers to your gourmet hideaway, weekend and evening programming is a good time in which to concentrate most of your spots. If you are using a station piped into offices, advertise on weekdays between nine and five. And do not overlook a popular station in a nearby city if your area draws people from that city for recreation or shopping.

Talk shows. Radio talk shows are a new means of helping to spread word-of-mouth recommendations for dining out. On this sort of program, people call in to a restaurant reviewer who discusses places to eat in whatever locale is requested. California radio stations have developed this format to the delight of the astute listening public, who have thus heard about countless places that might otherwise never have been discovered. Each format is different, but these reviewers cannot be bought. They give their own judgments of the places they visit; and then they allow callers to voice their own reactions on the air. You can have a friend help you get some notice by calling in to report on your place. But you had better be good—if you are not, it will be reported later by other listeners. So wait until your service and timing in the kitchen are down pat.

ADVERTISING FOLLOW-UP

Do not leave to conjecture the effectiveness of your advertising campaign. You must ask your customers how they happened to come to your place; don't rely on them to volunteer the information. Keep track of what sources are most effective, and spend your advertising dollars accordingly. If you must make a choice from among several local papers, you might try making some sort of special offer redeemable with a copy of the ad. Place the ad in two different papers. (The back of the cut out ad will be different for each paper.) You may find that both papers are closely read and do equally well in bringing business; or you may be surprised at the difference.

PUBLIC RELATIONS

The chamber of commerce. Join the local chamber of commerce. They will officiate at your "grand opening," which takes place at your convenience after your real opening. A photograph of the ribbon-cutting event always has the possibility of making the newspaper. You will probably be too busy to participate in chamber-of-commerce activities at first, but as a member you can have a voice to protect your business interests if something threatens your particular area, or restaurants in general.

Charity. A multitude of local and national charity appeals and other solicitations will be directed to you during the year. Though you cannot possibly contribute to them all, you can do certain things. You can offer gift-certificate meals to a selected few for use as door prizes or raffle prizes in fundraising campaigns. This sort of public contribution should be narrowly focused so as to limit your expenditures yet bring you the good will they engender.

Contribute to what is of genuine interest to you. Do you have children in school? Support school activities and limit other contributions; take an ad in the high school yearbook; or support parent organizations involved with youth activities. Perhaps senior citizens, the blind, or the mentally handicapped are your special interest. Whatever you do, use your business as a moral asset to put back into the community what you have taken out in another form. You may think you can't afford to contribute. In truth, you can't afford not to.

If your restaurant is dependent on transient customers, one of the tricks of the trade on a slow day is to have all employee vehicles parked in front of the place.

THE GUEST BOOK

A guest book offers two advantages, if you care to take them. It gives credence, of a sort, to what people have heard about your place. They see written evidence, created by people like themselves, of how good you are, before they enter the dining room themselves. In this way, the remarks in a guest book at the front desk serve as a sort of "point-of-sale" advertisement.

Second, it allows your guests to comment indirectly but effectively to the chef. It may not always be easy to take, but it is valuable. If you are doing things well, the remarks will reinforce your beliefs. If there are shortcomings, they may show up in the comments, or in the absence of comments. (Be sure your guest book has a column headed "Remarks.")

There is serendipitous entertainment value in such a guest book, too. There are always clever diners who will think of entries such as the following item from July 1976 at the Grey Fox Inn:

"Mr. & Mrs. Rex Sole, Halibut Drive, Abalone, Calif. The chicken was almondine!"

Or as one Oriental man remarked after ordering from our luncheon menu, which included mainly salads, sandwiches, and soup: "Questionable, no rice!" A famous feminist writer commented, "Interesting food and women." And a Mr. Hoffman was so enthralled with his meal that he took the guest book around to each table, introduced himself as Dustin Hoffman's father, and made everyone sign the book. Guest books are fun. And fun is the essential ingredient in life's recipe, especially when you are running a restaurant.

11. Prices and Profits

YOUR entire effort now focuses on whether or not you can make a financial success of your venture. Even if you are independently wealthy, your restaurant should show a profit for the time when you decide to sell it.

SETTING MENU PRICES

Dinner prices. The price of dinner at your restaurant should be determined as follows: multiply the wholesale cost of the meat portion by three, four, or five. Four is the norm. The multiplier you use will depend on what else is included in the dinner price. If you serve soup *and* have a salad bar, serve a relish or other appetizer, include potato or rice, and also serve a vegetable, then the higher factor may apply. If you serve a complete dinner including a beverage and dessert, you will be more likely to offer smaller portions of the main dish to avoid waste, and this may keep the price down. If you mainly use an a la carte menu where the patron gets to choose the side dishes desired, you may wish to price the main course a bit lower.

The wholesale prices of fish have been rising rapidly as

consumption increases and supplies dwindle. The multiplication factor has always been higher for a fish dinner because the spoilage rate is much higher for seafood and the labor of preparation is just as great as for most meats. If you are charging $8.95 for a dinner with a twelve-ounce portion of meat that costs you $3.00 per pound wholesale, you may very well decide to charge $7.00 for the equivalent portion of fresh fish that costs you only $2.00 per pound. More likely, you will serve a larger portion because the $2.00-per-pound fish is not a rich variety like salmon or swordfish, which are now luxury items, in the high-price dinner category.

Most restaurant critics will categorize your price range as moderate, expensive, or medium (in-between). You should decide what is the lowest price that the public ought to pay for a dinner at your restaurant and then try to have at least one menu selection at that price. If you set your median prices in the nine-dollar range, then one should be able to get a good dinner at your place for eight to eleven dollars. Add the price of a nice bottle of wine, tax, and gratuity to see what it will cost two people to have dinner.

The majority of American middle-class restaurant patrons would rather pay a little bit more for food that is really fresh, tasty, and beautifully served, than pay an average or "bargain" price for mediocrity.

If you allow your customers to order a la carte, your menu should differentiate the price of the full dinner from the a la carte prices. In a small restaurant on a busy night, you may be reluctant to serve just soup and salad to a table of young vegetarians. Set your a la carte prices accordingly. The hidden benefit on such nights, when a table wants just the main course without appetizer, soup, or salad, is that you make your normal percentage profit, but you will get the table that much more quickly for the next party. Most people, you will find, are interested in the full dinner menu.

The end price of the typical dinner should add up to what you and your local customers will consider to be a fair value for the amount and quality of the food. If you are facing stiff price competition, you will have to be satisfied at first with a lower profit until you are established.

There are many ways to ease the burden of eating out for people who appreciate fine dining but are on limited budgets. Serve "specials," in limited quantities, on the nights or days that are usually slow, or at times when the less affluent are willing to patronize your place. Or offer a price inducement to people who come for a meal early, when you would normally not be crowded, but your staff must be on duty anyway. For example, you might offer a discount on the second dinner for a party of two Monday through Thursday between 5 p.m. and 7 p.m. Although the profit on both meals is reduced, the increased cash flow pays the overhead, keeps the servers from getting bored, and keeps your suppliers treating you well because your orders tend to fluctuate less.

> *A person who simply hasn't enough money to leave any tip at all should either eat in a less expensive restaurant or order less. In Europe he would have no choice: a 15-percent service charge is automatically included in the final price.*

Portion size. Portion size is psychologically important in many parts of the country. If you are serving ranchers, loggers, or other hard-working people, you may wish to offer seconds to accommodate their tastes without producing too much waste with ordinary customers. But even that offer is ticklish to administer. You may have to have the server handle it rather than putting the announcement on the menu.

I have been asked many times why our menu does not offer a smaller portion at a reduced price. A few restaurants do make this a common practice, especially with steaks or prime rib of beef, for which it makes very good sense. But the price of the meal depends on more than the weight of the meat portion. A large percentage of the price must pay for labor and overhead. Obviously, these factors are exactly the same for each meal served, regardless of portion size. Most patrons do not realize this and are puzzled if the reduced price of a smaller portion seems still too high.

Breakfast and lunch prices. Breakfast and lunch prices usually do not have to reflect as many courses as dinner. Therefore, the price of a sandwich may end up being set other than by a rule of thumb based on the wholesale cost of the protein source in the sandwich. Remember, it is better to charge a little more and serve a sandwich that makes people at the next table sit up and take notice. If you add some little side dish that does not cost too much to prepare, but offers a contrasting taste and a pleasing setting on the plate, set the price to cover the added item. Junk foods, like soft drinks, are always higher-profit items. I am in favor of charging high prices for them to discourage people from ordering such poor foods, especially for children. Fresh fruit juices, on the other hand, are already expensive; anything you can do to hold the price down on those items will make you more popular. Your lunch or breakfast trade and the competition from other nearby places will, in the long run, determine your price range for these meals.

In the United States, coffee is the only restaurant commodity in wide demand for which most places charge a flat price regardless of the amount consumed or ordered and left uneaten. In Europe, coffee is a high-priced dessert item served by the pot. When the first pot is empty, you must order and pay for another.

The increases in the wholesale cost of coffee have focused attention on the American habit of offering unlimited coffee refills in restaurants. If you open for breakfast, you may find your small place filled with coffee drinkers who order nothing else. They sometimes take up space that would otherwise be occupied by bigger spenders. Your coffee policy is a personal matter. But you must consider several factors when you set the price of a cup of coffee. It might not be so bad for it to be too high for the "coffee sitters." On the other hand, it might not be wise to turn them away on the days when they might actually eat.

It is reasonable to have a minimum charge per customer on busy days. Do not be ashamed to make a good profit. You will have to work harder for it than almost anyone else I can think of.

When setting the prices of side dishes or a la carte items, take pains to do some simple arithmetic. If your regular menu offers a combination of items, be sure that the sum of the separate items' prices slightly exceeds the price of the combination. For example, if you serve a cup of soup with a sandwich and a beverage as a lunch special for $3.95, the separate cost of the same amount of soup and the same sandwich and beverage should be at least $4.15. If homemade pie is 90 cents per serving and a scoop of ice cream is 40 cents, then pie a la mode should be $1.25 or less.

Extra charges and specialties. There will always be customers who desire that some item not on the menu be added to a sandwich or salad. It keeps life from getting too routine. Be sure you post a menu in the kitchen so the staff will know the prices of such extras. When setting these prices, be sure to consider the added cost of labor in breaking the normal preparation routine, as well as the size of the added portion. Be reasonable and fair to both yourself and the customer. A small restaurant in our town antagonized many customers by deciding to charge an extra 25 cents to heat a sandwich. It was a foolish move, because it annoyed even those who never asked for a hot sandwich. People are willing to pay 50 cents extra for a slice of avocado, which they know is expensive, spoils quickly, and involves labor to prepare. But they rightly resent being charged too much for two minutes of heating in a microwave oven.

When you set the price of a sandwich, consider the size of the slice of bread on which it is normally served. If someone asks for a substitution of, say, your sourdough bread, which may have significantly larger slices, it could require 40 percent more filling to keep the sandwich from appearing skimpy. You might have to charge more if you cannot obtain different kinds of bread with similar-size slices. But do not nitpick. Some costs will simply average out over the year.

If you serve some very attractive specialty that is prepared in your kitchen, such as a special dessert or soup, or any other unique dish, be sure to charge a fair price that is not too low. Your actual labor costs may not be as great as the customer assumes, and your ability to ensure quality is inherent in the preparation, perhaps with a secret family recipe. If necessary, adjust the portion size to keep the price reasonable. One way to promote your special ability or idea is to offer small free samples to certain customers when you first introduce the dish. Let a few people in strategic locations know about your specialty, and soon the rest of the town will hear about it and come to try it.

Price increases. When you are faced with eroding profits due to wholesale price increases, there is a basic rule you must follow: maintain quality and raise prices. Your customers will understand. Do not wait too long to reflect your cost increases, either. If you do, you may find that the size of the increase will be too great. Smaller increases will be accepted much more readily, even if they are more frequent.

One side effect of raising prices is that you will have to alter your menus. It looks tacky to cross out old prices and use the menu over again. Therefore, design your menus so it is not too expensive to print new ones each time you change prices.

INVESTMENT AND RETURN

The initial investment to start a restaurant from scratch in a location that has not been equipped as such may come to as much as $90,000. You may do it for less, but you should have enough reserve cash to cover the rent for nine months to a year. If you are able to find a partially equipped location that needs little renovation, you may be able to start with a lot less. But a good location is crucial, even if the initial cash requirement is high; you will recover your investment.

Regardless of location, reserve capital is necessary to cover the likelihood of your making some costly mistakes during the learning and start-up period. You should plan on replacing at least one key piece of used equipment, which will break down within a month or two after you open. Unexpected new public building regulations may require some unplanned cash layout. Even if none of this occurs, you must be able to protect your overall cash and psychic investment in case some fluke circumstance temporarily affects your business. For example, just after you open at a very good spot on a main road, someone may take a notion to begin a nine-month street-widening project two blocks away. The ensuing dust, detours, and delays may divert traffic away from your place. Don't be discouraged. Those construction workers have to eat somewhere and they might come in if you visit the foremen to talk about your problem.

If you have more like $120,000 to $200,000 to invest, you should try to own your own building. Negotiate that option, if it is a possibility, in any lease you sign—before your business and reputation are well established and the landlord raises the price.

The annual return on your investment in a small restaurant is very likely to be small. If you are forced to borrow most of your starting capital at the current high interest rates, you will find most of your return going to debt retirement. That may be acceptable to you if you are building up equity in property that you are purchasing. If that is not the case, you should reconsider whether you can proceed without having the bulk of your starting capital free and clear. Most commercial lending institutions shy away from loans to inexperienced restaurant owners; and they are also reluctant to lend money on real property that has a single-purpose use, such as a restaurant, gas station, or bowling lanes. If you borrow money from friends, they must be made very aware of the high rate of failure for restaurants and of the time it will take for you to repay the loan. Do not borrow amounts from friends or relatives that they are not in a position to lose. Spread the risk by borrowing smaller amounts from more people. But do not give anyone a piece of the action unless you incorporate and sell stock, making yourself the controlling stock-holder. In a small restaurant there is never enough action for all the lenders.

Maybe you should go all the way and sell your home, if you have one, to raise capital. You won't be spending that much time there anymore, anyway.

> *What can you expect? You know that anything good will require you to put your heart and soul into it. It will take at least that, plus cash. The potential return is great personal satisfaction in your career, plus cash.*

The cash return can be figured fairly easily. Let us assume that you will have twenty tables, and you will serve two types of meals per day, six days per week, for eleven months of the year. If each table serves an average of five meals per day, at an average price per meal of $9 ($6 lunch, $12 dinner), then:

20 tables x 5 meals x $9 x 6 days x 48 weeks
= $259,200 gross income per year

If your profit after expenses is 12 percent of your gross, you should net about $31,000 personal income before taxes. If the net profit must be divided two ways, you can see that no one is getting rich with a small restaurant, though you should also keep in mind that your food costs at home will be lower. These figures may account for the fact that restaurants have the highest mortality rate of all small businesses. But what price do you put on satisfaction?

You may have fewer than twenty tables, or course, or a lower average meal price. The particular details of your price structure, restaurant size, and operating hours will all affect the gross income produced. But of even more importance are your expenses and overhead costs. If you can combine low building cost with careful use of labor, you ought to be able to increase your net income, and realize a net profit of closer to 15 percent. And if you can reach a level of quality and exclusivity that attracts the "carriage trade," you may even come close to an 18-percent net. But do not count on it, especially in these times of high inflation. If you decide to have only ten tables and serve high-priced meals, your net profit may still be low because labor and overhead will represent a higher percentage of the gross.

There are other ways of netting a profit than in dollars, though. If you value shorter working hours, you may find it possible to survive on only one meal service per day, which is most likely to be dinner. Or you may be able to work only four or five days per week, just like normal people. Even better than that, if you are in the right location, you might work like mad for nine months of the year, and take the other three to do the other things in life you want to do.

Restaurant patronage and cash flow fluctuate widely, especially if you are in a seasonal business area. The weather alone has a great impact on dining out. In our small town, where most people cook with electricity, the restaurants are jammed whenever there is a late-afternoon storm that causes a power failure. Since all restaurants use gas and the kitchen can be lighted with a camping lantern, the local people stream in to be fed, even in the semidarkness of candle-light.

Because of these fluctuations, it is imperative that you keep close track of your expenses and intake on almost a daily basis. Each week you should have a pretty good idea of your food and labor costs compared to your income. You can easily approximate the fixed overhead costs for the month and assign a weekly amount for that. The cost of food should be about 30 to 35 percent of your gross income from food for the week, excluding state sales tax, if any. (The markup on alcoholic beverages is greater, so figure it separately.) Labor costs, excluding your own and your partner's draw, should run about 33 percent. This percentage assumes you do not offer employees any special fringe benefits for which you pay directly, such as a health plan. It does assume that you will pay all the required state and federal benefits such as Social Security and unemployment taxes. (Your minor dependent children are exempt from these requirements.)

Your fixed monthly and yearly expenses should consume about 15 percent of your gross income. This covers:

- Rent or building payments, including property taxes.
- Utilities, including telephone.
- Fire and liability insurance, including workers' compensation coverage.
- Linen service.
- Maintenance and cleaning.
- Regular advertising.
- Permits, licenses, and special taxes.
- Trash and garbage removal.
- Office and administrative costs.
- Cost recovery (depreciation)
- Miscellaneous costs, for such things as soft water, gardening, extermination, special cleaning services, knife sharpening, bookkeeping, and dishwashing machine service.

There will be seasonal variation in some of these costs, such as those for linen, utilities, and advertising. Your insurance premium may be adjusted each year following an audit of your gross sales and your payroll. Also, inflation will cause your overhead to rise each year.

PAYING YOUR EMPLOYEES

If you employ most of your staff on a part-time basis, you can probably pay the federal minimum wage to those workers who earn tips. Since kitchen people do not get tips, you will have to pay them more, except perhaps during a short initial training period. The prevailing wage for kitchen workers in 1982 was $5 to $7 per hour, depending on the responsibilities assigned, although the job market in your area may allow you pay even less. (Federal law even allows for trainees to be paid less than minimum wage for a short period, by prior written agreement.) Food preparation workers are rarely paid enough. Most restaurant employees know this, and those who accept food prep jobs often expect to move up to server positions as soon as possible. A few small places spread the wealth either by rotating people in both kitchen and dining room jobs or by pooling all tips and allocating them on some basis to all employees. Each system has drawbacks.

Employee compensation practices vary in the restaurant business. Nonunion wages for servers and buspersons are typically set at the minimum required by state and federal law. The busperson who does an excellent job usually gets 15 percent of the tips received by the server. You should establish a clear policy on that subject rather than rely on the good nature of your servers. Since the busperson has easy access to the tip on the table, a dishonest or dissatisfied busperson is intolerable. Even the mere suspicion that tips are being "ripped off" will immediately destroy the morale of the dining room staff.

Employee meals and benefits. The Public Housekeeping section of the Federal Minimum Wage and Hour Act is very clear about what you may and may not do in making deductions from employee wages. By prior written agreement, you may deduct from their wages the cost of meals and lodging. But you are not required to provide meals to your employees. If you do, you must pay Social Security tax on the value of the food, using a government-set amount for breakfast, lunch, and dinner. It is to your advantage, however, to provide meals to an employee who works a long enough shift to need a meal. In addition, since dishwashers are typically underpaid, it is common to provide at least one hearty meal per shift.

As mentioned earlier, it is a good policy that employees should arrive at work not expecting to eat immediately. After four hours, they should get a meal and a break. Federal law requires a half-hour break after five hours, unless the shift is over after six hours. The intensity of effort required at a busy restaurant often works against having time for even a bathroom break for periods of two or three hours. Common sense and caring among your staff members will establish reasonable practices for helping everyone get through the day without an accident.

Other fringe benefits, such as paid vacations, are not practical to offer when your staff has a high turnover. It is simpler to call the money a bonus and to pay it just before the restaurant closes for vacation. You can establish whatever incentives make sense for bonus eligibility, such as length of service. I have heard of restaurants that actively promote the sale of desserts or wine with bonuses as a reward for the server who can achieve above-average rates.

Group health and hospitalization insurance is nice to provide; but you may not be able to afford it along with workers' compensation coverage. Group life insurance is not necessary. However, you may wish to offer your people the opportunity to purchase their own health and life insurance at a group rate through the restaurant. (You will thereby get your own personal insurance at a lower rate also.) This usually requires the participation of at least ten people for an entire year, and most small restaurants do not have a permanent staff of that size. You will also incur administrative costs. Check with a reliable insurance broker who has written coverage for other groups. Then compare the information with the coverage obtained by another small group in your area.

Losses through the back door. I must now discuss a distasteful subject that has a direct bearing on your profits. People steal food from restaurants. Employees do it. Friends of employees do it. In a sense, even you are doing it, if you take food that your partner does not also take. Not only do the culprits take food, but, being connoisseurs, they may also wish to have a nice glass of wine or beer with it. If your food costs are exceeding 35 percent of your gross income, and you cannot account for it through spoilage and analyzing your menu prices, then the food is going out the back door. No one is likely to break into locked storage, although it does happen. But the availability of keys to your storage and kitchen must be closely restricted.

Quiet security consciousness is the answer. If you deal honestly with your employees, losses of this sort will be kept to a minimum. If you catch anyone, deal with him swiftly and decisively. If you are a softie, you are being dishonest with yourself and your other employees, who depend on your staying in business for their livelihood. Change your locks occasionally.

12. What About Automation?

IS THERE a place for electronic data processing (EDP) in a small restaurant? To answer this question, you first must understand that computers and data processing systems have evolved significantly in recent years. The changes continue at an astonishing pace, even as I write this, threatening to moot the question before publication. What follows may include some unfamiliar data processing terminology, but you may as well get used to it. Your children and friends are already using computer jargon, which serves the same purpose as the argot of the restaurant business—that is, it makes communication with co-workers easier.

Today you can carry in your shirt pocket a computing capability that not long ago would have required equipment the size of a typewriter. Fifteen years ago a complete data processing system consisted of a central processing unit, a main memory, and peripheral equipment such as magnetic tape drives, a line printer, a keypunch console, and a punched-card reader. All of this was installed in a large air-conditioned room with a raised floor to hide the cables and to channel air used to cool the equipment. A system with equivalent computing capability is today housed in a desk-sized rack and needs no special installation or cooling. Current systems handle ten times the data at five times the processing speed and are sold for less than one-tenth of what a system cost ten years ago.

the data at five times the processing speed and are sold for less than one-tenth of what a system cost ten years ago.

These advances have been made possible by miniaturization of computers through silicon chip technology. Using the same technology, the modern cash register has become a true "point of sale" system, rather than merely a complex adding machine with a cash drawer.

WHY SHOULDN'T YOU HAVE IT EASIER TOO?

What does all this have to do with serving good food? The enemies of quality include fatigue, waste, fraud, confusion, and inefficiency —all of which can abound when you have too much to do with too little time available to do it. Though smallness makes possible the managerial control necessary to maintain high quality, smallness alone does not prevent these enemies from invading your operation. Nor does it ensure that they can be driven out as you gain experience.

Someone has combined the smallest pocket calculator with a small plastic tray for delivering a guest check and credit card form to the table for signature. Now the diner can check the arithmetic of the bill and easily compute a tip at whatever percentage suits the occasion. The thing costs less than twenty dollars.

A small data processing system, tailored to your needs, can probably offer you the means to neutralize the enemies of quality. You and your well-trained staff can assure quality without the aid of special equipment, of course, but to do so you need certain essential data about your operation, which take time to assemble. Your time is limited. The less often you examine your operation using these data, the more likely you will not discover the waste, fraud, and inefficiency that destroy your profit and thereby your ability to continue to offer excellent service.

So whether or not you believe that you can afford one of the newer systems for restaurants, it is important for you to know just what is possible. It is well worth a closer look.

YOUR RESTAURANT IS A SYSTEM

Assuming that you have an ordinary operation, let us begin by looking at the point where the most important data are entered in your restaurant system. This occurs when a server takes a customer's order and writes it on the order form. Does it surprise you that I refer to your manual operation as a system? It *is* a system, you see, even if the only equipment you use is pen or pencil, order pads, an adding machine, and a cash box.

Inputs. For the system to start, it needs to be told what specific food and beverage items the customer desires. The ancillary data written on the order are used for managing the process. They include how main dishes are to be prepared, table number, name of server, date, number of persons at the table, and possibly other information, such as whether special-offer prices apply. All this information is called "system input."

Timing. Separate copies of the multiple-part check allow transmission of the input both to the kitchen and to the source of beverages and side items, which may or may not be assembled by the server. A one-part order form requires the server to run back and forth or else to have a good memory. It is important that the kitchen staff know how far along the customers are in consuming the items that precede the main course. The chef must know when to start each cooked-to-order main course so all meals at a table can be served simultaneously, neither too soon nor too late. The chef must also consider the overall order of preparation for all tables so as not to make one party wait longer than others.

Outputs. Food and service are not the only outputs of your restaurant system. Another vital output is the bill presented to the customer. This bill is often the same form used for input, with the prices entered and totaled, including tax, if any. Some restaurants produce a guest check separate from the input order form, especially if they have a cash register with special printing capability.

System problems. This is what can happen (and has happened) to the order form containing all that important input.

- If the handwriting is sloppy, it can be misinterpreted.
- It can become temporarily lost, stuck behind another order form or in a greasy crack.

- Additional items ordered can be omitted from the guest check, especially if the server can provide the item without going through the chef.
- When prices are inserted or the total added, sizable errors can occur.
- When checking the bill, the customer may find it difficult to read or understand it.

Solutions. In previous chapters I have mentioned the importance of legible handwriting and a smooth and efficient relationship between servers and kitchen personnel. If there were a system that eliminated those problems by providing the following, would you use it?

- When the server enters data at a keyboard in the dining room, the exact order, including all ancillary information, is printed in the kitchen, where the chef and others can easily read it.
- Orders for beverages are printed at the location where they are prepared, also with ancillary data.
- Throughout the meal, the system remembers all information entered at the keyboard, including additions or substitutions.
- At the end of the meal, at the press of a few buttons, a straightforward check is printed in plain English, listing all items served with the correct price for each, and the correct total amount including taxes, even if the tax rate varies with the type of item. The arithmetic is never wrong.
- The system records the method of payment—whether cash, check, or credit card—including the amount of any gratuity added on the charge slip.

There are obvious advantages to having all this information readily available to the staff members who need it. Elimination of arithmetic errors alone can have a surprising effect on profits. But some advantages of such a system are unexpected. One of the best is this: the server times the entry of data for each course according to the progress at the table. With this scheme, all items that appear on the kitchen printout are prepared as soon as possible thereafter. Thus, the chef is relieved of the stressful chore of juggling the main course preparation times for the entire restaurant. The timing of meal delivery is now almost entirely in the hands of each server.

Another advantage is that the server no longer has to memorize prices. Yet another is that at the end of a shift, upon pressing a few buttons, the manager learns the total amount of tips owed to that server from charge slips. The server's name and the amount is printed on a slip, which the server signs as a receipt to the owner in exchange for cash. This feature enables easy compliance with the tax rules for reporting tip income. It also allows the server to go home sooner.

Management Aids. It is to the manager that such a system offers the ultimate time-saving advantages. Employees record their arrival and departure for each shift via the keyboard, and from this input the system prepares payroll. Throughout a day's operation, information about any table is at the manager's fingertips for monitoring progress or checking, for example, on whether the order for an expensive bottle of wine—or a second bottle of wine—has been entered in the system yet. If the manager wants to know how many meals of a particular type have been served, this information, too, is easily obtained via the keyboard and printer. Would the server like to know how many meals she served, or how many dollars worth of meals, for whatever reason? Push a few buttons, but only after the system has been put into the "manager's confidential mode" by use of a key or entry of a secret password by the manager. This mode restricts access to information that rightly should be available only to those with a "need to know."

Beyond the convenience of no longer having to go through the day's receipts, checking for errors in arithmetic, looking at the mix of meals served, and generally examining the day's results, the EDP system gives the manager immediate access to specific information about the operation that is otherwise difficult to extract. The time thus saved can be used to better advantage in training employees, thinking of new ways to serve good food, or just enjoying the work.

COMPUTERS NEVER GET BORED

Regardless how sophisticated a system you get or what computer programs you use with it, your managerial skills will be enhanced by the EDP system's two main advantages: accuracy and speed.

Accuracy. First, all your arithmetic calculations will be accurate. If the system reports that your gross sales for the week were $25,000, the amount will not be wrong because of a slip of the finger on your adding machine. If you ask the system to figure your labor costs as a percentage of gross sales, you can expect the report, no matter how often you request it, to show the correct amount, based on actual hours worked by your staff. Similarly, if you desire to know what percentage of gross sales each type of meal on your menu represents, and how this percentage compares with the relative cost of each type, you can rely on the accuracy of the reported figures, assuming that you have entered into your system the basic data needed for such calculations.

Speed. Second, generating the kinds of reports just described will hardly take longer than the time needed to switch the system to "confidential" mode, ensure that the right report-generating program is in the computer, request the printout, and watch it emerge. The time needed to produce the same reports manually is normally so long that the small restaurant owner or chef rarely has at hand the vital information such reports provide.

EDP systems for large food service operations are advertised as "providing management control that allows you to compete with small restaurants." This may come as no surprise to the veteran small restaurant chef who can tell almost to the penny how much profit is made from a menu item on any given day. But why shouldn't this overworked chef also have the daily, weekly, and monthly summary reports available at the touch of a few buttons, so that he or she continues to be tough competition for the big guys?

NOTHING IS PERFECT

Let us assume that you are willing and financially able to go further —that you are interested in a system to fit your planned operation. What should you do about it? In the past few pages I have painted a somewhat rosy picture of the advantages offered by a restaurant EDP system. To begin, you must first examine what can go wrong. Your EDP system is just as vulnerable a part of your operation as the chef who becomes ill, the power supply that fails, the dishwashing machine that breaks down, or the exhaust system that burns up. All these subsystems are much less likely to break down and interrupt the smooth running of your restaurant if they are periodically checᴋ. and serviced (yes, even the chef!). Someone must do preventive maintenance and replacement of worn parts, and unless you are unusual, it won't be you who does it.

Fortunately, computer programs cannot wear out. They *can* become obsolete, but more on that subject later.

Local service. Electronic and mechanical parts that comprise EDP equipment are subject to failure. Sometimes they wear out. More often they are affected by mishandling or power fluctuations. These ills are preventable with proper electrical safeguards and good training of the staff. Although the number of moving parts in current EDP equipment is surprisingly small, even microelectronic elements occasionally need replacement. Just as you do for your dishwashing machine, you will have to depend on a local person or organization to fix your EDP system.

The importance of having local service available at all times cannot be overemphasized. Your system will not wait to "crump" on a slow Monday. It will stop dead at two-thirty in the afternoon during Mother's Day dinner when your waiting room is so full, people are overflowing onto the sidewalk. Clearly, your EDP system service must be available on all weekends and holidays.

Backup capability. When the dishwashing machine breaks, you do your best to wash dishes well enough by hand to continue operations until the repair service arrives to fix it. Much the same will occur with your EDP system, with one significant difference. People don't forget how to wash dishes by hand. Your dining room staff, especially, will become so dependent on the EDP system to do all I have heretofore mentioned that they may find it difficult to carry on without it. In a small restaurant it is easier than in a big one to drill the staff for such emergencies. You may wish to wait to install your EDP system until you are sure you have a smooth operation without it. Or you can operate without the system at least one day per week for a month or so, until you are convinced that the staff can handle emergency operations manually.

Choosing a dealer. Clearly, when you are first considering what system to buy and from whom to buy it, prompt and reliable service should be a top requirement. If you are located in a remote area, your chances of obtaining quick service are not great. But if you are anywhere in a major metropolitan area, you have an excellent chance of finding an EDP dealer–service organization whose representative will be happy to discuss your particular case and advise you on what type of system would be suitable for your restaurant.

If you happen to be in the New York–New Jersey area, make it a point to contact Michael Shulman at Restaurant Control Systems, Inc., in Union, New Jersey. No, Mr. Shulman is not a relative of mine, nor is he a business associate. But I have found him to epitomize an attitude exhibited by the suppliers of all sorts who serve restaurant owners best. He knows his products; he understands and appreciates the restaurant business; he devotes his full attention to the customer's problem; and he is more interested in being reliable and maintaining his reputation than in selling products of any particular brand. Besides that, he loves to eat. What better recommendation could you wish for?

More EDP dealers coming. As automation of restaurants spreads in the United States, the Michael Shulmans of the industry will become more numerous, even in the less populated areas. Look for the qualities he exhibits as you make inquiries, listen to presentations, and read literature on various systems. The dealer who is already well-established will invite you to see systems in operation in restaurants. Spend the time it takes to observe and learn, and ask the same kinds of questions of the staff that I recommended you ask when viewing other restaurant kitchens (see Chapter 2). It doesn't matter if the restaurant is small or large.

A systems service organization may not limit its work to restaurants, since any number of retail businesses can use similar equipment with differing software. A new company may be just getting started in your area to provide the service you need. That shouldn't rule them out. The key to choosing your EDP adviser is whether he or she has both restaurant experience and demonstrated knowledge of systems analysis. Ask to see resumes of those who purport to advise you. Honest, smart businesspeople may well give you a good deal because yours will be one of the places they'll show proudly to other potential customers.

HOW MUCH IS THIS GOING TO COST?

Don't be surprised if the dealer wants to show you everything before discussing prices.

Prices can scare you away. At this writing, you could easily be facing a price tag of $15,000, plus additional amounts for installation and training and for the yearly service contract. But though labor for producing computer programs and documentation and for training is not getting cheaper, equipment prices are going down. If trends are not overcome by inflation, the total cost for a system may soon be reduced by 30 percent or more. You should be able to buy a basic start-up system, including installation and training, for under $10,000. Considering today's prices for cash registers and the savings you'll realize through elimination of errors, you may find that the system will pay for itself, so to speak, within a few years. So, I agree with the dealer—don't let a high-sounding price prevent you from investing the time needed to learn what's what.

> *In the next few years, it is possible that an EDP system suitable for a restaurant or other retail business will retain a higher resale or trade-in value than other restaurant equipment in the first two years after purchase. EDP systems don't get greasy. They fit into small corners. And computer programs can be brought up to date or adapted for other functions. But a reach-in refrigerator is always just that. Besides, computer hardware is fast becoming so inexpensive that an EDP system may soon be as cheap as a refrigerator.*

Leasing. The suppliers of any new product for the restaurant industry must take into account that their customers often start up with insufficient capital. For years, soft drink and beer suppliers have been leasing out equipment to ensure sales of their "consumables." The consumable in your EDP system is repair and maintenance, and possible installation of equipment to modernize your system or expand its capability. By all means, explore terms for leasing an EDP system with your supplier-dealer, but before you do, discuss the tax, legal, and insurance implications of such a lease with your accountant, attorney, and insurance agent. These discussions should help you formulate questions to ask the dealer when you negotiate the terms of the lease. Bear in mind that equipment manufacturers sell equipment. If you don't buy a system, someone else has to before you can lease it. In times of high interest rates, the cost of money added in the lease price can make it less cost-effective to lease than to take advantage of tax reductions through cost recovery (depreciation) of owned equipment.

Used systems. Judging from past trends in both the small restaurant business and the small computer business, those of you in major metropolitan areas may have the chance to get a used system from a closed restaurant. If so, better handle it through the service dealer, just as you would have a competent service shop check out a used refrigerator you wanted to buy. Used EDP equipment must be suited to your operation, not outdated, and still capable of providing years of satisfactory service. Your dealer may also know of a small system that has been replaced by newer equipment in some recently expanded restaurant. Be very cautious about such a system. If it is not obsolescent, perhaps the dealer will be willing to sell it *and service it*, with a satisfactory guarantee, at a price that would make it worthwhile.

WHAT DO YOU GET WITH YOUR EDP SYSTEM?

A dealer or manufacturer's representative will assume that you know a lot about the restaurant business but little about data processing. You'll probably receive the thorough explanation you deserve, therefore, with most or all of your questions answered before you ask them. So that you will better understand your supplier's explanations and their implications for a small restaurant, however, I will tell you what questions should be answered, why they should be answered, and what the answers will mean.

System components. A restaurant EDP system capable of performing the functions I have mentioned consists of a computer, one or more data entry devices—that is, keyboards, sometimes called terminals, similar to those on typewriters or modern cash registers—one or more printing devices to provide information to the kitchen and elsewhere, another printing device suitable for producing guest checks, and a terminal that is connected to the cash drawer. It is not necessary for the cash drawer to be directly connected to the system, but the cash will be protected this way, as it would be with a cash register.

The aforementioned equipment is collectively referred to as "hardware." Before discussing the essentials of "software," that is, the computer programs, you need to know more about the computer.

Computer. The computer is the component that is able to interpret the instructions and the data needed to accomplish the system functions. It is also the component that controls the other, "peripheral," units like the printers and the terminals. Some computers are now so small that they fit in the same case that holds the terminal keyboard. A computer this small is called a microprocessor. It can be contained in a single silicon chip or in several. The part of the computer in which the instructions and the data are stored is called the main memory. (More on memory in a moment.) The computer in a restaurant system is most likely to be a minicomputer (which is small but not so small as a microprocessor), or possibly several microprocessors, or a combination of computing components.

Ask your dealer to show you the actual computer in the system proposed for you. Yes, make him open the case, so that at least you will understand what it looks like. Also ask to be shown what parts of the unit can be replaced without taking it back to the shop. Ask how much the spare parts cost and how long it takes to find an error, locate the faulty part, exchange it for a new one, and test to see that the system is back in working order. This way you will better understand just what your service contract means and why it costs what it does. Don't be surprised if one of those chips the size of your fingernail costs more than a day's profit of your restaurant.

Memory. The computer also must have a magnetic storage component, called a memory. In the memory is stored the computer program, which is the series of instructions that cause the data to be processed as desired and the information to be stored and printed as called for. Also in the memory are the data unique to your restaurant or common to any restaurant operation. It is important for you to know whether the type of memory in your system holds data even when the power is temporarily shut off. If it doesn't, the system must have a battery that switches into operation the instant there is a power failure. Such a backup power capability is especially important for a restaurant. In the event of a power failure you will need to continue your operation at least until the customers present are served and have paid. And the electrician needs time to get there after you call. If the power problem is outside the building, the backup power gives you time to get ready to use the manual procedures that you have practiced so well. Remember?

Bits and bytes. Information in the memory is stored as "bits," and eight bits make up a "byte." If your computer has a capacity of 8,000 bytes, it is said to have an "8K" memory. Or it could be 16K or 32K in size. If memory capacity is large enough to allow all the computer programs and the data to fit into the main memory, then each program is easier to design. But it is also desirable to be able to have computer programs and data stored in a record that you can carry from place to place without taking the computer along. Such records are called "auxiliary memory" units. In the past, wide magnetic tape was commonly used for this purpose, but it is not suitable for small systems. Diskettes or cassettes, which are similar to the audio magnetic storage units we know as LP records and tapes, are also used for computers. By storing your computer programs and business records for the month to date on a small flexible disk, also called a "floppy disk," you can actually lock these important assets in a fireproof safe. It might be important to have on hand an extra copy of the program tailored to your operation so you can load it into the computer right after the repairperson has fixed the system on a busy night. As you may have guessed, it is possible for a breakdown to disturb the memory to the extent that its contents are all jumbled up and rendered useless.

If the power in your area is subject to fluctuations or anomalies that can affect computers, you may have to install a "power conditioner" to ensure that your data and software are protected. The hardware normally is already protected.

Computer programs. By now you have figured out that it is the computer program that makes possible all those time-saving and error-free operations mentioned earlier. The company that supplies the EDP system has analyzed restaurant work and created programs especially suited to it. Your computer program is a series of instructions which, when loaded into the memory with specific data from your menu, such as the names of dishes and the price for each, cause the EDP system to respond to entries made at the keyboard terminal.

Special programs, using the data entered in the memory while you are serving meals, produce the reports mentioned earlier.

It is not really necessary for you to be able to read a computer program or to understand exactly how it is created. You already have enough to do. You must understand that your computer is capable of working with various programs, not only the ones provided with your system. This means that it is possible to change or expand your system later on so it will be able to do more than it did at first. It also means that if an improvement in the standard programs is dreamed up by a programmer at the factory, you should be able to get the improved program for your system, too. And it should be provided at little or no cost.

Software. The term "software" is used to describe the computer programs, the training manuals, and other printed material that describes what your system should do, how to test it, how to fix it when it breaks down, and so on. Often the term "software" is used in place of "computer program." So if the dealer tells you that "new software packages" or "updated software" will be provided to you free of charge, he means that the manufacturer will send out improved computer programs that were not previously available, along with manuals that describe how to use them.

To make it easier to describe them in the remainder of this chapter, I will adopt the popular terms used in the trade for the two general types of restaurant computer programs. "Front-of-the-house" programs make possible the transactions needed to handle food and beverage service, collect payments, and perform the activities that are ongoing during regular operating hours, such as employee time clock, tips summary, and so on. "Back-of-the-house" programs provide reports and planning information for management, perform accounting tasks such as payroll, and provide other important services, but are not normally used during hours when you are open for business.

Auxiliary memory devices. You may need more memory capacity than is available in your system's main memory. As mentioned earlier, the diskettes or cassettes serve for storing extra copies of computer programs and vital, confidential business data that must be safeguarded. In addition, if your system can use diskettes or cassettes, your main memory does not have to be big enough to hold both front-of-the-house and back-of-the-house programs at the same time. After a day's operation, when you are ready to run back-of-the-house programs, you simply transfer the program from auxiliary memory to main memory (where the front-of-the-house programs have been operating) and process the management reports you need. The front-of-the-house programs that were in main memory are simply written over by the incoming back-of-the-house programs. This is just like what occurs when you record something on an audio cassette that already had something recorded on it. When you go back to regular restaurant operations, the front-of-the-house programs must again be "read into" main memory from auxiliary memory.

In a similar fashion, your daily totals will be added to a running record of your business and stored in a diskette or cassette for later use in the back-of-the-house programs that prepare your accounting and tax records, payroll, and other management reports. Your dealer will train you to handle the auxiliary memory devices for such purposes. During your training, it is important to ask how you will bring your cumulative records up to date after each day's operation, and how you will keep them accurate when the system breaks down and your staff works by the old manual system that they have practiced so well.

The terminal keyboard. I have already noted how easily new software can be introduced to your system. It is an inherent characteristic of computer programs that they are adaptable. This is not true for hardware. For instance, once the physical layout for a terminal keyboard is fixed, it cannot easily be revised. If the push-buttons are arranged in 10 rows of 14, you have 140 push-buttons available for use in entering data and operating your system. But whereas the 10-by-14 array is permanent, alterations in the software can change the effect of pushing a particular button. This means that buttons labeled with all your menu items for front-of-the-house program operation can have an entirely different set of labels for use with back-of-the-house operations. To make the exchange easier, the push-buttons themselves are not labeled; rather, you are supplied with a plastic overlay that fits over or around the entire keyboard and shows new designations for each button function. Obviously, the overlay in use must always correspond to the computer program in memory. To understand better what I mean, think of this parallel situation: the latest electronic typewriters can be used to type in different languages using different alphabets. When you change the alphabet character disk, you must also change the keyboard labels to match, or else each key must be labeled with two or more characters from different alphabets.

It makes a lot of sense to get a keyboard designed to be impervious to liquids. Not only do servers sometimes have wet fingers, they also sometimes spill the liquids they are carrying. Why take the chance that such a slip will put your system out of service?

The keyboard overlay and the corresponding software must be tailored to the changing needs of your particular restaurant and menu items. Be sure that you understand exactly how your system will accommodate changes—not just in prices, which may occur relatively often, but also when you want to add, delete, or modify items. Other labels, some of which may not actually be spelled out on the keyboard, change too. For example, if your employees are assigned codes with which to identify themselves whenever they make a system input, a list in the computer software must identify each code with an employee's name, and possibly social security number. The system will refer to this table when it acts as a time clock and performs other functions that concern individual employees. Before you choose a system, you should fully understand exactly how this list of codes, and other such important and confidential system data, are safeguarded and modified when necessary.

Printing. When your business records are kept in books and ledgers, it is simple to check on their current state; you just have to look at them. When your records are stored in magnetic form in a computer rather than in ink on paper, you have an entirely different situation. It is easy, of course, to have the system print out on paper the contents of a diskette or cassette. But how do you know what period of business is represented by the data in the record? When dealing with magnetically stored data, you must diligently label your tapes or disks with the date and contents. Otherwise you run the risk of inadvertently destroying irreplaceable data, using out-of-date data and merging it irretrievably with composite records of business, and creating a mess of data the likes of which you would never be able to explain to the IRS auditor. A well-designed system will include a feature that identifies every magnetically stored file and prints out the identifying code along with the contents of the disk. But you must understand how this feature works and how it might be unintentionally bypassed. And you still must label the cassettes or disks so that you don't waste time using the wrong one. A good system design will allow you to check the contents of a record by its identifying code before you actually run a back-of-the-house program.

You should ask the dealer how the system prints out the identifying code, and if it always appears at the beginning (and perhaps also at the end) of the printout. Having the date and time printed at the beginning and end of every report could help you avoid terrible mixups, especially when you run a report again after some inputs have been corrected. This would assist your accountant, too.

Some systems print the time of day along with the date on guest checks. Be sure that the time-of-day feature can be suppressed, upon request, because some businesspeople would be embarrassed if the boss (or the spouse!) were to notice an odd time of day on a bar bill.

It is a good idea to have your accountant become familiar with your proposed system before you are committed to install it. He or she will be interested in the audit trails and features that will affect the business records needed for compliance with tax regulations and for other accounting purposes. For example, you may have a lease or other financial obligation that is tied to your gross sales. Your accountant may be able to suggest a special software feature that could be added to your system at no great cost, to help you figure the amount owed. Possibly, your accountant will find that a back-of-the-house program can reduce the number of work hours required for your monthly recordkeeping. He or she will at least make sure that a program is accurate and performs as advertised. If your accountant is not already familiar with restaurant EDP systems, he or she should become so, or you should get an accountant who is.

THERE ARE LESS EXPENSIVE WAYS

What I have described so far is a system capable of doing perhaps more than is really needed, and at too high a cost, for the owner of a small restaurant. I will now describe a minimal system, consisting of only a register with a relatively simple keyboard and a connected guest check printer. With this type of system, which costs about $4,000, two basic functions can be partly automated at a lower initial cost. The system has a microprocessor within the register, but it does not permit selection of various computer programs. Its fixed program, contained in a memory permanently stored inside the equipment, is not easily revised. There are also now available, or soon will be, various options with costs and capabilities lying between those of the extremes described here.

Eliminating arithmetic errors. The minimal setup will enable you to eliminate the errors servers often make when totaling the guest check. The register is capable of storing in its memory up to three hundred different menu items, with prices for each. The server specifies the desired food or beverage by entering on the keyboard a three-digit number that represents it. For the convenience of the servers, the menu is posted above the register with the proper number for each item clearly visible. After entering all items desired at the table during a particular course, the server pushes another button, which causes the register to produce a two-part order slip from a two-inch-wide paper roll. On each half of the order slip is printed the name of each item (in abbreviated form) along with its price. The two halves are divided by a perforated line, with the date and the server's identification number on each. The microprocessor determines the price through a function called "price look-up," often abbreviated "PLU" in the trade. The same function is used to print the guest check.

Guest check printing. One of the best features of the expensive system previously described is often called the "retained check function." This enables the system to keep an internal record of all items ordered at a particular table, so that at the end of the meal the guest check can be printed at the press of a button. Since information in memory is easily changed with this system, it is possible to void any errors and to record changes in a customer's order so that the final guest check is uncluttered and clearly readable. With the simpler system, the server has more work to do each time another course is ordered. And the more entries the server must make, the greater the chance of making an error.

The simple system does, however, help the server avoid most errors. It works like this: When a server wants to order items, he or she must insert a passkey in the register. The server's number is then printed on all slips he or she requests. When the items have been entered and the two-part order slip has been produced, the server inserts the guest check in the printer, and the same items and prices are printed on the customer's bill. If the server forgets this step and removes the passkey without inserting the guest check, a tone sounds to remind the server to complete the transaction. Until he or she has done so, no other server's key or entries will be accepted by the register.

Since the system's memory does not retain the subtotal for each table, it is up to the server to enter the prior subtotal before adding newly ordered items. The server reads the prior subtotal from the guest check, and enters it along with the sequence number printed beside it. This allows the register to check the subtotal entered at the keyboard against the amount recorded for that sequence number in the system's memory. If they are not the same, the alarm tone sounds.

The system then prints the names of the new items, their prices, and a new subtotal. After a many-course meal, the guest check produced by this system is cluttered with many subtotals. To help the server position the guest check for proper printing at each transaction, line numbers are preprinted in the check's margin.

Controlling flow of orders. The two-part order slip provides a means of controlling how and when orders are sent to the kitchen or beverage area. The order slip pops up from the register and is automatically cut from the roll. The server writes on the slip the table number and any special instructions such as cooking style or substitutions, and takes it to the kitchen or beverage dispenser. When items are delivered to the server, they are accompanied by half of the two-part slip. This is kept by the server for reconciliation at the end of the shift. The other half is retained by the kitchen or bartender for cross-checking against the server's shift total. The slips can also be used to update inventory.

For this system to work well, it is necessary for the server to have easy access to all her guest checks. If the server must carry them all in a pocket, it is too easy to hurriedly pull out and enter items on the wrong table's check. With this simple system, unfortunately, the only way to void an entry is to manually cross it off the check. Of course, the end-of-shift reconciliation must also void the amount involved. To avoid such errors, it's best to have a rack, labeled with each server's name, where checks can be slipped into slots (similar to a time card rack near the punch clock). This takes up space and can be unsightly unless hidden from the dining room, but it makes it easier for the server to see the table number at the top of the guest check. It also makes it easy to arrange the checks in the order in which parties were seated or main courses were ordered. These manipulations make the server's job much more complicated than it would be with the retained check system.

Advantages and drawbacks. The simpler system provides one of the main advantages of any EDP system: it allows you to shift control of meal preparation sequencing from the kitchen to the server. It also eliminates the arithmetic errors that occur when employees have to look up prices or read sloppy handwriting. It offers the means for stricter control of what goes to the table; that is, if an item served isn't printed on the guest check, a discrepancy shows up between the total dollar value of items ordered by the server (an amount that is calculated automatically by the system) and the total of all the server's guest checks. This last total must be figured manually at the end of the shift, using the register as an adding machine. When a discrepancy cannot be accounted for by voided items, the source of the error must be found. Usually, the server is accountable for items omitted from the guest check. Such omissions are not possible with the retained check system, because the same actions that produce the order slip cause every price on it to be added to the stored totals for that table.

The main disadvantage of the simpler system is its lack of any significant back-of-the-house functions. At the end of the day, the manager can have printed out the percentage of total sales represented by each of up to nine different categories of menu items. This is something, but not much. Since the keyboard on the register is not very versatile, even the entry of new six-character abbreviations for menu items becomes an exercise in ciphering. There are no alphabetic keys, so the letters must be encoded using the numbers one to twenty-six. This may be bothersome, but it works.

The lack of flexibility in the simpler system and its limited memory capacity are the very characteristics that contribute to its much lower price. The question for the small restaurant operator is whether the advantages that it offers, in comparison with both a fully manual operation or the more expensive system, are worth the cost. As the dealer is very likely to point out, if your alternative is a cash register, the simple system offers advantages that will soon pay for themselves.

INITIAL COST VERSUS LIFE-OF-THE-SYSTEM COST

When your dealer shows you several restaurants with differing systems, be sure to ask the managers what additional costs besides the monthly service charge can be attributed to operating the system. Also, ask those managers who have had systems in operation for several years to give you some idea of how the annual costs have varied over time. The answers to these questions will help you assess which type of system you can afford. There are other considerations, too.

Price considerations. When comparing systems, do not look only at the initial costs for hardware and software. Be sure to get a clear understanding of what these changes cover and how much the monthly service contract will cost, both before and after the manufacturer's warranty expires. Who pays for spare parts and for correcting software errors? Also, be sure you understand how the training for you and your staff will be paid for, and to how many hours of training the price entitles you. You must learn to operate the system, but you must also be sure that you can easily train others to do so. Because restaurant employees change jobs often, you cannot afford to rely on the dealer to train your new people. Be sure the system has a training mode, in which keyboard entries are just for practice and do not affect business data files. When visiting other restaurants, find an opportunity to ask members of the staff how long it took them to learn to use the system.

Try to get an idea of the likely cost of future improvements to the software or hardware for the system. If you want to take advantage of new developments or expanded capability offered by the manufacturer of the smaller system, you will very likely have to pay for them, especially if they involve any hardware adaptation. New software packages for the larger, more flexible systems, however, are more likely to be offered to you at little or no cost. With the simple system I've described, you have the option of attaching a remote printer that you could place in the kitchen. If you think that this printer might be useful in the future, despite the fact that it will print neither table number nor special instructions (since these must be handwritten), be sure that you get the basic register designed for easy connection to such a component. Otherwise, should you decide later to get a remote printer, you will have to pay for any electronic modifications needed.

It is commonplace for experienced servers to resist learning to use a new system. A waiter who had worked for thirty years in a restaurant that uses the simple system described here was adamant about not wanting to learn the new ways. Today, he is the one who is the most upset when the system breaks down.

Other trade-offs. Some differences between systems are not easily assessed just by comparing price. The time and energy spent by servers in movement to and from the kitchen is a hidden cost, especially in larger premises. In a small restaurant where servers already must go to the kitchen to grab salads, ladle soups, and assemble desserts, the trip to the kitchen to deliver an order slip may represent only a small percentage of the total transit time. However, small restaurants often have small kitchens, where any reduction of traffic will add to efficiency of operation. Thus, the system that substitutes the server's trip with the speed, accuracy, and convenience of an electronically transmitted message permits the servers to be assisted by a single kitchen helper, who prepares all items the cook does not and passes them to the servers. The key to efficiency here is that a few motions by the server at the keyboard are translated into a permanent record and a usable printed order in the kitchen without requiring much movement in the work area. The time thus saved can be used to improve service at the table, which can increase the usage rate of tables—that is, improve "turnover"—if that is a goal for your place. Or it may allow three servers to do the work formerly done by four—a definite saving in labor cost. Or the servers may simply be less tired and more friendly. Such advantages are possible only if your system allows all necessary information to be entered at the keyboard and automatically printed in the kitchen or beverage area.

Compare service costs, too. When deciding between two levels of system capability, be sure to question the dealer closely about the differences in cost of monthly service. Using the rule of thumb that system maintenance costs are about 10 percent of the purchase price per year, the less expensive system should be truly cheaper after ten years of service than the higher priced system. But since the cost of maintenance and emergency repair service is based partly on the time needed to travel to your place of business and find the fault, the rule of thumb may not hold true in both cases. First, the travel time would be the same for either system, and, second, the more expensive system may have built-in fault isolation and test capabilities that allow the repair to be completed in less time. So the prices for the two service contracts may be nearly equal. If this is the case, the difference in total cost between the two systems won't be nearly as great as would be indicated by simply comparing the initial purchase prices.

Keep in mind that the foregoing assumes you will not upgrade either system for ten years. This assumption may prove to be a naive one in today's world of technological advances.

> *The decision to install an EDP system may open new possibilities when looking for the right location for a small restaurant. You may be able to move into a building that has too little room on one floor for both the dining room and the kitchen. By planning to use a reliable system along with an old-fashioned dumbwaiter, you may find that a very efficient operation is feasible. Such a building may offer something special to the diner, such as a fine view of the city or landscape, or something special to the owner, such as a lower price per frontage-foot.*

A LOOK INTO THE FUTURE

The hardware innovations that have taken place in the years 1972 to 1983 presage significant changes for restaurant EDP system. To help you understand what this means for you and how it should influence your decision to install a system, I would like to make some predictions. Time will prove me either too optimistic or not bold enough.

Changes in terminals and keyboards. The newer systems will dispense with keyboard overlays that label the functions of the keys according to which back-of-the-house programs are operating. The terminal will have a multicolored screen that displays an image of the special function keys at the bottom of the screen, just above the actual special function keys. When you select a group of special functions, the terminal will display the appropriate key labels for you. This feature will enable you to use your system for an unlimited range of functions. I will describe next some of the kinds of services that you may have available.

Use of the display screen. When a multipurpose display screen is incorporated in the terminal, every output from the system can be checked for completeness and correctness before printing. This means that the server can make all entries and then check them before having the order printed out in the kitchen or bar. The same is true for the guest check. It is the manager who will reap the greatest benefit from this feature; he or she can now quickly view all reports on the screen before they are printed. Those daily or hourly reports that are of only immediate interest will never have to be printed at all, especially if the information contained in them will be incorporated in the monthly summary. The amount of paper to be printed and filed will be significantly reduced.

All printed material needed in the restaurant will be produced by the system, possibly in more than one color of ink. The material will include, for example, menu sheets, notices for employees, special instructions for key personnel, and order forms for various suppliers. For those messages that do not actually have to be printed on paper, the system will store them in memory for call-up at any time. The system will also notify the employee that a message awaits.

Cost trends. The price of such flexible "intelligent" terminals will be so low that for the price you would pay today, you will be able to have a terminal with display screen at every significant work station in the restaurant. This means one in the storeroom for inventory purposes, too. But you will add costs for telephone communications if you take full advantage of future area network services.

Linking your system to the world. The manager of the future will spend part of the work day shopping—while sitting at his console. This is already technologically possible by use of an acoustic coupler, which, when an ordinary telephone receiver is placed in a special cradle, connects your computer to the phone system. The future system will not tie up your telephone receiver, but it will tie you into restaurant suppliers' data bases in which are recorded all the items available, with delivery dates and prices. The distributors of food, beverages, and all other supplies will be vying electronically for your business, and brokers will describe comparative prices and quality via your display console when you seek special items or bargains. Once you decide what you want, a push of a few buttons will not only order the goods, it will also electronically debit your business bank account and credit the supplier's account. If, after delivery, you're not satisfied with the goods, your refund will be made in the same way.

If the restaurant's system is linked to the manager's home computer, the manager will not have to be in his office to do this work. It can be accomplished at home, in the middle of the night, if need be.

The "intelligent" terminal with display screen will make possible the use of software that completely trains new employees, or all employees when new functions are added to an existing system. Not only will the system explain itself to the trainee, it will provide exercises and evaluate the way the trainee handles them. It will even include suggestions for improvement or timing. It will invite the trainee to ask questions; upon request, it will review information already presented or offer another way to look at it. It will probably even reward quick learners with the opportunity to play the latest electronic games for the remainder of the learning period.

Innovations at the table. Eventually, entries into the system may be made right at the table. Tiny transmitters and receivers, whose radio frequency and range are limited to the restaurant interior, will replace wiring. This will allow the server to wear a featherweight keyboard on the wrist. As the server stands before the customers, he or she will enter the order as it is given. The system will know from which server and at which table the order originates, thus eliminating the need for entering those two pieces of data. A radio signal emanating from the table will encode the table number; it may even determine the number in the party by the weight on, and the temperature of, the chair seat. The system will recognize which server made the order because each server's wrist transmitter will be assigned a separate frequency. So no one can ever make an error by entering the wrong table or server identification number. And the manager's wrist keyboard will be the only one on which special service can be requested, such as complimentary drinks or dessert.

WHAT DOES ALL THIS REALLY MEAN?

Is your head spinning? With everything else you have to contend with in planning your restaurant, who needs future shock? My point in all this is simply to inure you to the accelerating rate of change in EDP systems. You may have to plan on changing your system or methods more often than you will renovate your restaurant. More often than you will buy new refrigeration—a lot more often.

But you will not need to do so unless the investment is cost-effective and your competition is reaping benefits from newer systems that result in lower prices or better service to the customer. These trends are already affecting other businesses dramatically. It remains to be seen how soon they will strike the small restaurant operation.

13. What to Do If . . .

PREPARE yourself for the unexpected, the unusual, and the worst. Find the nearest emergency hospital, and the most competent medical practitioners in your area. (They are probably among your patrons, if you have a fine dinner reputation.) Post a telephone list where it will be most readily used to call an ambulance, the fire department, the police or sheriff, and the rescue squad. Make connection with a competent attorney. Place your insurance with a local firm that can serve you in person rather than by phone or mail, and add the agent's number to your emergency telephone list.

Anticipate building emergencies. Keep handy the telephone number of the man who services your automatic fire extinguisher system. Find a reliable electrician and plumber who will give emergency service on weekends, and have them inspect your building to become familiar with the layout. You may need the services of the person who operates a sewer-pipe reaming device. Locate and mark all the available waste pipe cleanout fixtures. When a sewer line clogs or your exhaust fan motor burns out in the middle of a busy Saturday night, you must have someone available who will not tell you to wait until Monday morning.

PEOPLE EMERGENCIES

People emergencies are inevitable. Eventually, someone will become ill or be injured in your restaurant. Someone will fall down the stairs, or trip over a loose spot in the carpet. An employee will cut himself on a sharp knife or piece of glass. In dealing with these events you have only to follow a few simple rules:

- Remain calm and talk in a low, even voice.
- Give specific directions to people who can assist.
- In serious cases, call the rescue squad at once.
- Perform first aid competently, and notify a doctor.

If possible, move the victim out of the dining room into an area where he or she can be isolated from the public. It is best, however, not to move a person who may be seriously injured. In such cases, first aid and comfort should be administered without regard for unavoidable onlookers. In a small restaurant, a medically trained person present will usually identify himself and offer to assist. The proper first aid for choking, burns, severe bleeding, coronary episodes, and other common acute medical emergencies should be known to you.

Everyone who works in a restaurant should know how to perform the Heimlich Maneuver (or "manual abdominal thrust") as first aid for choking victims. It is illustrated on the following pages. Choking is one of the three most common causes of accidental death in the United States; and when people drink alcoholic beverages, eat meat, and talk too much, the danger of choking is increased. In California restaurants a poster describing the procedures must be displayed where employees can study it. You should try to arrange for a paramedic or other qualified person to demonstrate cardiopulmonary resuscitation (CPR) and first aid for obstruction of the air passage to you and your staff.

If a foreign object or substance is accidentally present in food served to a customer, you should know what to do. Someone may break a tooth on an inexplicable piece of gravel, or cut his tongue on a piece of glass. Your liability insurance for "completed operations" will cover these cases. Instruct your servers to take the injured person immediately to the rest room or kitchen and to call you. Sometimes hysteria will result from such unfortunate occurrences, and you should know how to calm down and treat the victim.

Once the victim has been given proper treatment, it is time to make a record of the date and time of the incident, the names of witnesses, and other pertinent facts for your insurance report. Make no contentions regarding negligence. Simply record what happened as best you can and promise to report it to the proper agency. Do not argue with anyone, especially within the dining area. Let an air of calm assurance prevail, even if you are very upset.

Be sure your kitchen first-aid supplies are kept current. If an employee is injured, you should be able to provide adequate treatment and protection for a minor wound. Burns should be kept under ice water for at least five minutes. For anything more serious, such as a bad burn or a cut that might require stitches or that will not stop bleeding, you should insist that the injury be examined by a doctor or that the victim go to the emergency room of a hospital immediately. Many employees will not want to do that, but it is necessary for your own protection in case of later infection or complications. Your workers' compensation insurance will cover the cost of medical treatment, and state laws require that such injuries be reported.

BUILDING EMERGENCIES

Fires are preventable. Invite the local fire inspector to check out your premises each year. He may save you a lot of grief. But if a grease fire does occur, even if you have an automatic fire extinguisher system or sprinklers, you should try to put it out with a large hand-held carbon-dioxide extinguisher kept in the kitchen. The carbon-dioxide extinguisher offers the advantage that it does not harm food that is sprayed with it. Most of the automatic systems, in contrast, have two disabling effects on your kitchen. First, they cover everything with a fine chemical dust that is inedible, so the food must be discarded. Second, they automatically trip a valve that shuts off the gas supply to the kitchen. Before you can cook again, the valve must be reset by your fire-extinguisher serviceman.

If a fire does set off the automatic system, you will probably have to shut down for the night, or suffer at least a several-hour delay. If your fire-extinguisher serviceman is available immediately, and not too much food was ruined, you may be able to get going again after the gas-line valve is reset, which takes a short time. Discuss the procedure with the serviceman when he installs your system.

FIG. 2

Maneuvers for Relieving Foreign Body Obstruction

Three maneuvers are recommended for relieving airway obstruction: back blows; manual thrusts (abdominal thrust or chest thrust); and manual removal of foreign bodies (tongue-jaw lift and finger probes). The technique for each of these maneuvers is described below, and the recommended sequence of maneuvers is described in the following section.

BACK BLOWS

Back blows are defined as a rapid series of sharp whacks delivered with the hand over the spine and between the shoulder blades. The blows may be administered with the victim in a sitting, standing, or lying position. The back blows should be applied quickly, forcefully, and in rapid succession.

Victim Standing or Sitting (Fig. 2)
1. Position yourself at the side of and slightly behind the victim.
2. Deliver sharp blows with the heel of your hand over the victim's spine between the shoulder blades.
3. Place your other hand on his chest to support him.

Do not just pat him on the back; use a series of hard blows.

Whenever possible, the victim's head should be lower than his chest to utilize the effect of gravity.

This page is reproduced from "First Aid for Foreign Body Obstruction of the Airway," a booklet published by the American National Red Cross.

MANUAL THRUSTS

This maneuver is defined as a rapid series of thrusts to the upper abdomen or lower chest that force air from the lungs.

The Abdominal Thrust
Victim Standing or Sitting (Fig. 5)

1. Stand behind the victim and wrap your arms around his waist.
2. Place the thumb side of your fist against the victim's abdomen, slightly above the navel and below the xiphoid process (tip of breastbone).
3. Grasp your fist with your other hand and press it into the victim's abdomen with a quick upward thrust.
4. Repeat if necessary.

FIG. 5

The Heimlich Maneuver (or manual abdominal thrust)

This page is reproduced from "First Aid for Foreign Body Obstruction of the Airway," a booklet published by the American National Red Cross.

If you should have a dining room fire, or if someone ignites his clothing or your curtains with a cigarette, try to put it out with a hand-held extinguisher of the proper type, which should be kept in or near the dining room. Your carpeting and drapes should be resistant to flame; but your linens will not be. It is imperative that all ash trays be dumped into a container not used for paper or dirty linens. Many kitchen fires result from sloppy handling of ash trays that still contain embers.

When an electrical failure cuts off power to your building, you should be ready to continue as best you can under other types of artificial light, such as battery lights, camping lanterns, candles, or kerosene lamps. Some jurisdictions now require emergency lights in the dining room and kitchen to allow safe departure during a power failure by the public and the employees. If the interruption of power is within your building and you cannot solve it by resetting the circuit breaker, your must get your electrician to come right away. The same is true for plumbing trouble.

ROBBERY AND BURGLARY

Discuss the subject of armed robbery with your local police. If you have any large amount of cash on hand on a weekend, you could be a target, especially if you are in or near a high-crime area. Ask how best to protect the lives and property of your customers, your employees, and yourself. Then issue instructions to those who regularly or occasionally operate the cash register. Become familiar also with the methods used by quick-change artists, who usually try to work their scam on young employees who have to make change at the cash register. You and your staff should also learn how to recognize counterfeit money.

If you discover significant amounts of food or supplies or any equipment missing, whether or not there is evidence of a break-in, report the facts to the police. If food and supplies are disappearing, take a close look at the methods you use for issuing supplies from storage and for controlling access to locked areas. Hold a staff meeting to discuss the problem, and ask for suggestions from your employees on what to do. If you suspect that the culprits are local people, or even friends of your employees, work with the police burglary expert to apprehend them.

BUSINESS SLUMP

If you are keeping close track of your business, you will know when you are beginning to get into financial trouble. Do not wait for your accountant to tell you the bad news. Respond to a temporary loss of business by immediately reducing your labor costs as much as possible and by really cutting down on waste. Prepare to offer and advertise some good specials if the slump continues. Make some small but noticeable changes in your dining room or out in front of your building. Even a fresh coat of paint or some new attraction in the front windows will cause people to take notice and want to see what is going on inside. Consider bringing in some special entertainment on certain nights. If times are hard the cost may be lower than you think, and you can always offer to pay in part with food.

If the slump persists, you should consider getting a professional analysis of your operation and of the problems you are having. The Small Business Administration (SBA) can offer some advice. But there are also volunteer organizations of retired businessmen who remain active by helping other small and medium-sized businesses to be successful. The local SBA office should be able to direct you to one of these groups. This kind of counseling is available at little or no cost and can provide invaluable advice and encouragement to help you turn things around. All of these steps should be taken while you are still operating in the black or close to the break-even level.

BIG TROUBLE

Even after taking over as much of the work as you and your partner can handle yourselves, and after determining that your prices are right and no one is stealing your food, you may not have enough business to turn a profit after expenses. You have a hard choice to make: relocate, try to sell the business, or cease operations. The real reasons for your restaurant's failure may be very basic—your personality, your reputation, the limitations of your overall menu and dining room design, or some other problem too big to correct.

Relocation. It rarely makes sense to relocate when you are in business trouble. An exception might be if you have the chance to get a nicer place in a more convenient spot, perhaps even at the same or lower cost; or the chance to buy rather than rent a building. Your long-term lease arrangement may discourage you from making a move at all under your existing business name. But if you are close enough to your old location for your name to be worth transferring to the new one, you will merely be moving your troubles to a different spot. If an independent analysis shows that in fact you could do better at another, available location, however, and your operation is basically sound, the trouble of moving might just be worth it. It will not be easy.

Selling out. Even if you decide to move, you might consider selling your equipment and the lease to someone else who wants to try to make a go of your present location. If you plan to relocate your business, you should retain the right to your name, of course, and you should not sign any noncompetition agreement that would prevent you from opening at the new location. Or, if you are retiring from the restaurant business, you can sell your name as well.

List your business with a reputable broker, who will tell you what you are likely to net from a sale. You may have to ask a much lower price than you would like, especially if all you have to sell is your equipment, your leasehold, and a business that is barely making a profit. However, during hard times there are often people who feel shaky about their positions in industry and who have some small savings that they think it wise to invest in a small business. One may come along who believes he can do better than you did.

When you look back on it all, don't cry . . . smile.

Closing. If you have allowed the business to dwindle in value to the point where no one is willing to buy it, then you have essentially a worthless business and some valuable equipment. Your lease may be worth something, depending on whether someone could pay the rent by operating a different kind of business in the building.

You will want to get as much for your equipment as possible. If you are not in or near a major city, you may have to call in a used equipment dealer or auctioneer to offer you whatever he thinks it is worth. Get bids on the whole set of equipment from as many dealers as you can. If you are in a city, you may find it better to advertise the equipment yourself and to try to sell the larger items without having to pay any commission.

There is some advantage, though, to having everything sold in one day. Therefore, it may be best for you to hold an auction right on your premises conducted by one of the reputable auctioneers in the area. Make sure it is advertised well and held on a good day for local restaurant people. If you are in a small town, it may be best for you to hire someone to haul your equipment to the nearest large city that has restaurant auctions and dealers. Do not hurt your back moving anything. You will be especially vulnerable to such injuries as you see your pride and (former) joy dispersed.

You should also confer very closely with your accountant and attorney about what steps to take to protect yourself from claims that could hold up the sale—by creditors, the state, or the federal government. Your attorney can explain to you the advantages and disadvantages of voluntary bankruptcy proceedings.

On that somber note I conclude this book, adding only these few final observations. Nothing is forever. You may create the finest small restaurant in the state. It may give you the greatest feeling of accomplishment and security you have ever known, despite the incredible amount of hard labor and devotion it demands. But someday you will find that it is time to change the locks on your security, or someone will try to take it all away from you—by offering to buy it, or by opening up next door with a new idea. Or you may lose a negligence suit over something that was not your fault. There are no guarantees in the restaurant business, or in life. The only true security is in doing your best at whatever you choose to do. The real adventure is always at a risk. Are you alive? Go on, open your little restaurant. To say, "I once thought about opening a restaurant," doesn't count.

Index